Editor
Lorin Klistoff, M.A.

Editorial Manager
Karen J. Goldfluss, M.S. Ed.

Editor-in-Chief
Sharon Coan, M.S. Ed.

Cover Artist
Sue Fullam

Art Coordinator
Denice Adorno

Creative Director
Elayne Roberts

Imaging
James Edward Grace

Product Manager
Phil Garcia

Publishers
Rachelle Cracchiolo, M.S. Ed.
Mary Dupuy Smith, M.S. Ed.

STANDARDIZED TEST PRACTICE FOR 1ST GRADE

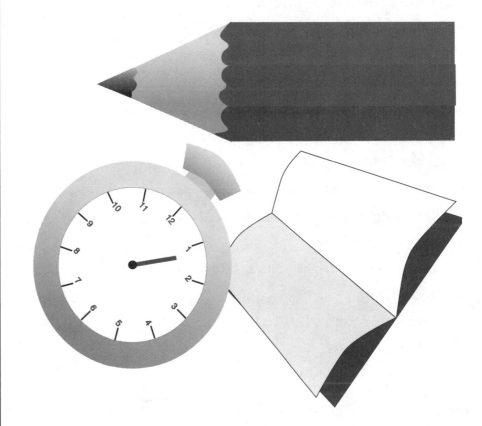

Author

Charles J. Shields

Teacher Created Materials, Inc.
6421 Industry Way
Westminster, CA 92683
www.teachercreated.com

ISBN 1-57690-676-0
©*2000 Teacher Created Materials, Inc.*
Reprinted, 2003
Made in U.S.A.

Table of Contents

You have undoubtedly given plenty of tests during your years of teaching—unit tests, pop quizzes, final exams, and yes, standardized tests. As a professional educator, you know that standardized tests have taken on an importance greater than any of the others.

No one who understands children and the nature of learning would argue that a standardized test provides an absolute measure of a child's understanding, a teacher's effectiveness, or a school's performance. It is merely a statistical snapshot of a group of children on a particular day. And there is no "generic child." Take a look at a girl named Joanna, for instance. Reluctant to speak during discussions or participate in group work, she's a whiz at taking tests and scores high on formal tests. However, Dion, in the seat beside her, is creative but impulsive. He dawdles during timed tests and sometimes fills in the wrong answer section. His score? It is no more a true indication of his ability than his doodles of motorcycle-riding monsters in the margins of his papers. You are probably thinking of a Joanna or a Dion in your class right now.

However, schools must be accountable to their communities. Moreover, issues of equity and opportunity for children require that some method of checking all students' progress as objectively as possible be administered annually or even semi-annually. As a result, at the insistence of parents, school boards, state legislatures, and national commissions, standardized tests and their results are receiving more attention than at any other time during the last 35 years.

The purpose of this book is to help you and your students get better results on standardized tests. The exercises are grade-specific and based on the most recent versions of these testing instruments:

The California Achievement Tests
The Iowa Tests of Basic Skills
The Comprehensive Tests of Basic Skills
The Stanford Achievement Tests
The Metropolitan Achievement Tests
The Texas Assessment of Academic Skills

Exercise materials designed for this book reflect skills from curricula, grade-level tests, and test taking from the California Academic Standards Commission, the New York State Testing Program for Elementary and Intermediate Grades, the Texas Essential Knowledge and Skills program, and the Board of Education for the Commonwealth of Virginia. Your students can expect to meet again on widely used standardized tests most of the content in this book and the style in which questions are posed.

About the Practice Tests

You will notice several things right away about the exercises.

1. The tests are arranged by curricular topics: word recognition, whole numbers, or geography, for example.

2. The exercises are short enough that you can integrate them into your teaching day. If, during the several weeks prior to the test date, you spend 20 minutes on test taking, your students will build confidence and increase their knowledge base in preparation for the actual test. Becoming familiar with testing formats and practicing on sample questions are effective ways to improve scores.

3. Examples of student-constructed responses to problems and questions have been included. Students must write, draw, or show their work to get credit for their answers.

The first two sections of the booklet—Practice Listening and Practice Guessing—emphasize skills young children need to know to be good test takers. The other sections are divided according to subject area—Language Arts, Mathematics, Science, and Social Studies.

Ways to Increase Students' Confidence

- Downplay the importance of how many right answers versus how many wrong answers your students give. These exercises generally have the same purpose as drills in sports—to improve players' ability through regular practice. Fill the role of coach as students learn to hit the long ball.

- Give credit for reasonable answers. Encourage students to explain why they answered as they did. Praise thoughtfulness and good guesses. Surprise them by giving partial credit because their logic is persuasive. On some state-designed tests, credit is given for "almost-right" answers.

- Promote a positive, relaxed feeling about test taking. It might be wise, for example, to put off administering a planned practice from this booklet if your students are anxious or feeling overwhelmed about something. Use a little psychology in strengthening the association in their minds between test taking and opportunities to feel pleased about themselves.

The following pages provide a list of the basic skills embedded in the tests in this book.

Language Arts

Phonemic Awareness

Blend the phonemes of one-syllable words.

Segment the phonemes of one-syllable words.

Count the syllables in a word.

Change the beginning, middle, and end sounds to produce new words.

Decoding and Word Recognition

Use sound-letter relationships to decode one-syllable words.

Recognize common irregularly spelled words.

Use punctuation, syntax, and sentence and story meaning to decode one-syllable words.

Spelling and Writing

Write all the uppercase and lowercase letters of the alphabet.

Use phonics and patterns to spell three- and four-letter words.

Apply phonics to write independently.

Use basic punctuation and capitalization.

Language, Comprehension, and Response

Read and comprehend narrative and expository text.

Elaborate on how information and events connect to life experiences.

Predict and explain what will happen next in stories.

Understand the concept of a sentence.

Respond to what, when, where, and how questions.

Mathematics

Whole Numbers

Count using one-to-one correspondence.

Make sets; match numerals.

Identify ordinal position.

Conserve numbers.

Read and write numerals 1–10.

Recognize one more/less and before/after/between.

Compare and sequence numerals.

Count by rote ones, twos, fives, and tens.

Make reasonable estimates of how many.

Group objects into tens and ones.

Represent numbers in a variety of ways.

Solve problems using addition and subtraction.

Use counting strategies to find sums and differences.

Geometric Ideas

Identify plane and solid figures in the environment.

Use directional and positional words.

Identify likenesses and differences.

Mathematics (cont.)

Classification and Pattern

Sort by attribute.

Continue patterns.

Find and correct errors in patterns.

Identify patterns in the environment.

Measurement

Compare objects.

Use nonstandard units to measure.

Identify unequal parts.

Use time-related words.

Name and order days of the week and months of the year.

Use the information on a calendar.

Tell time to the nearest hour.

Identify the values of pennies, nickels, and dimes.

Problem Solving

Solve spatial visualization puzzles.

Estimate reasonable solutions.

Copy simple designs.

Science

Process

Make observations based on the five senses.

Classify objects according to their properties.

Use amounts as a means of quantifying.

Estimate length, volume, mass, and temperature.

Make inferences to form conclusions.

Make predictions.

Social Studies

Individuals and Families

Identify roles of individuals in the family.

Distinguish similarities and differences among people.

Identify social environments.

Compare social environments.

Describe appropriate behaviors in various environments.

Authority and Responsibility

Identify individuals who have authority.

Recognize consequences of responsible and irresponsible actions.

Religious and Cultural Traditions

Identify religious and secular symbols.

Identify symbols associated with holidays.

Geography

Locate familiar places in the home, classroom, and school.

Identify functions of places in homes and schools.

Analyze patterns of movement between homes and schools.

Why Practice Listening?

The purpose of the "Practice Listening" exercises is to introduce students to the multiple-choice format of testing. Tests at this level of school are very similar to the exercises in these pages. The tests contain many choices—usually pictures—with a circle under each picture. Children at this age usually do not fill out name grids nor do they have to pace themselves against the clock. The script you read aloud is their guide to the test and how long they should spend on it.

Incidentally, it is a good idea not to overly emphasize neatness or complete erasures. Children at this age should be learning to listen, to concentrate, and to evaluate. For now, neatness is not a priority.

Answers to most test questions at this age have to do with the context of the pictures. A sample question might be the following: "Which of these children are swimming?"

Questions with absolute answers, such as 20 x 4 = [?], are asked more frequently on tests for children in third grade and higher.

One of the biggest listening challenges first graders face is becoming adept at integrated listening. Integrated listening on a test will require them to listen to a question containing key words such as *only*, *between*, *under*, and *unless* while simultaneously examining possibilities. This is the next step up from simple identification of the right answer.

Turn to the "Here's the Idea" exercise on the next page.

Here's the Idea

Read the script below to the children. The exercise introduces students to the practice of choosing one answer.

Teacher Script

In school, children take tests. Why? The reason is that your teacher, your parents, and the school leaders, such as the principal, all want to know more about what you are learning in school.

They can tell partly from your seatwork and partly from your work on the bulletin board. However, a test has its own, special purpose. A test will check what you know and how you think. A test gives teachers and parents clues about how to help you in school. It is important you try your best on a test.

Open your book to the page with four animals. *(Check to see if students are on the correct page.)* Do you see the four pictures? What do you notice about them? *(They all have four legs; they are all animals.)*

Which is the only animal for riding? *(the horse)*

When you take a test, you get a book like this. Your teacher reads a question to you like I just did. You listen to the question. You decide which choice in the row is the right answer. Then you fill in the little circle next to your answer. If I put a circle on the board, who can show me what do to the circle on a test? *(Have a student fill in a chalk circle on the board.)*

That is right. You fill in the little circle near the horse.

But what if you fill in a circle and change your mind? *(You erase it.)* Let's practice erasing. Fill in the circle under another animal, not the horse. *(Pause.)* Now pretend you changed your mind. Erase the wrong one.

It is all right to change your mind. Just make sure you erase the wrong answer and fill in the one you think is right.

Let's practice taking a test. Turn the page.

Try and Discuss

Read the script below to the children. This exercise introduces students to a sample test and gives the students a chance to discuss their answers.

Teacher Script

This is what a test looks like. Pictures are in rows. The questions I will read to you are about the pictures. You choose the picture that answers my question.

Look at the row that has the number 1 beside it. Put your finger on the number 1. (*Make sure students each have their finger on the correct place.*) This is the row of pictures I am going to ask a question about. Listen while I read the question. Which one flies in the wind? Fill in the circle under the picture you choose. (*Pause.*) Which circle did you fill in? (*the one under the kite*) That one was easy, wasn't it? Maybe you knew the answer right away.

Now, look at the row that has the number 2 beside it. Put your finger on the number 2. (*Make sure students each have their finger on the correct place.*) This is the row I am going to ask you a question about. Listen while I read the question. Which is the slowest? (*Pause.*) Which circle did you fill in? (*the one under the turtle*) Sometimes you must compare the choices to see which one you think is right.

Look at the row that has the number 3 beside it. Put your finger on the number 3. (*Make sure students each have their finger on the correct place.*) This is the row I am going to ask a question about. How much is 1 + 1? (*Pause.*) Which circle did you fill in? (*the circle under 2*) This time you knew there could be only one right answer. You did not have to compare very much, did you?

Now, put your finger on the number 4. (*Make sure students each have their finger on the correct place.*) Here is the question about this row of pictures. Which animal is the fastest? (*Pause.*) Which circle did you fill in? (*the one under the horse*) But wait! These are the same pictures as before. What is the difference? (*You asked for the "fastest" this time.*) Good listening is listening carefully.

Look at the row that has the number 5 beside it. Put your finger on the number five. Listen while I ask you a question about this row. Which one grows the fastest? (*Pause.*) Which circle did you fill in? (*the one under the flower*) All of these things grow, but the last one grows the fastest. That is why you must look at all the pictures before choosing just one.

Now, put your finger on the number 6. Listen while I ask you a question. Which is the only girl with a scarf? (*Pause.*) Which circle did you fill in? (*the third one*) But there are two children with scarves. Why did you choose the third one? (*Because you said "girl with a scarf."*)

You must listen to every word in a question.

ANSWER KEY

1. kite   **2.** turtle   **3.** (2)   **4.** horse   **5.** flower   **6.** girl with scarf

---

1.

    ◯   ◯   ◯   ◯

2.

    ◯   ◯   ◯   ◯

3.   **1**   **3**   **2**   **4**

    ◯   ◯   ◯   ◯

4.

    ◯   ◯   ◯   ◯

5.

    ◯   ◯   ◯   ◯

6.

    ◯   ◯   ◯   ◯

Practice Test

Read the script below to the children. This exercise gives the students a chance to practice listening by completing a sample test independently.

Teacher Script

Now you are ready to take the practice test on listening. Remember to listen carefully. We will not stop to talk about each question this time. I will ask the question, and you will fill in the circle of your answer. Then I will read the next question. *(Answers appear in italics and at the bottom of the page; you can discuss answers with students at the end of the test.)*

Put your finger on the number 1. Has everyone found the number 1? *(Check to make sure students each have their finger beside the correct row.)* Which person is having something to drink? *(Pause.)* *(the second one)*

Put your finger on the number 2. Which picture has only animals in it? *(Pause.)* *(the third one)*

Put your finger on the number 3. Trisha said, "I like small dogs best." Which picture shows Trisha's favorite kind? *(Pause.)* *(the fourth one)*

Put your finger on the number 4. Gabriel said, "I lost my baseball. Now I can't practice." Which picture shows the ball Gabriel lost? *(Pause.)* *(the first one)*

Put your finger on the number 5. Manny drew a circle on a piece of paper. Then he drew two more shapes. Which picture shows Manny's paper now? *(Pause.)* *(the second one)*

Put your finger on the number 6. Which picture shows two rows of two? *(Pause.)* *(the second one)*

Do you see the stop sign at the bottom of the page? That means stop.

Do not turn the page.

ANSWER KEY

1. person drinking something (second picture) **2.** animal group (third picture) **3.** smallest dog (fourth picture) **4.** baseball (first picture) **5.** paper with a circle, a triangle and a square (second picture) **6.** two rows of two (second picture)

1.

○   ○   ○   ○

2.

 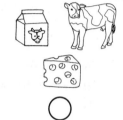 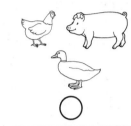 

○   ○   ○   ○

3.

○   ○   ○   ○

4.

○   ○   ○   ○

5.

○   ○   ○   ○

6.

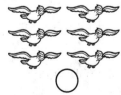 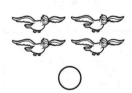 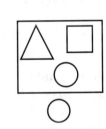 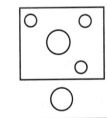 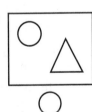 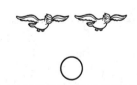 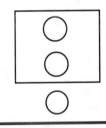 

○   ○   ○   ○

Why Practice Guessing?

Sometimes students will not answer a question on a test because they do not know the answer. Faced with choices that seem similar, they opt for no answer rather than choose a wrong answer. A second reason students will leave a question blank is because the material is unfamiliar to them. In this case, students may think they do not know enough to make a choice at all.

Learning the process of elimination teaches students to rely on what they do know. The key to the process is finding information in a question or set of answers that is meaningful to the student. Students may not know what an igloo is, for example, but they can recognize a picture of an ordinary house and a doghouse—those cannot be igloos!

The questions in this section are slightly beyond a first grader's ability level. The purpose is to confront students with a term or a concept or a set of choices that is hard to understand. Emphasize to them that standardized tests are not usually this hard. Explain that they are learning how to get rid of answers that cannot be right.

In fact, it is not important that students choose the exact right answer to each question in this section. The goal is to get them to eliminate two obviously wrong choices. Two right answers will be given for each question in the teacher's script. The better answer of the two right answers will be underlined. It is a good idea to go over the questions and answers in the tests right away to reinforce students' understanding of how the process of elimination works.

Here's the Idea

Read the script below to the children. The exercise encourages students to make good guesses at correct answers by using the process of elimination.

Teacher Script

Sometimes you have to guess on a test. You may think, "I don't know the answer to this question," or "I'm not sure of the answer." But you should always answer every question. You might have to guess. We are going to learn how to make good guesses.

We are now going to play a guessing game called "Which Animal Is the Most Popular at the Zoo?" This is how we play. I will think of an animal. Then I will give you clues. You will listen and cross out the animal that cannot be the one I am thinking of. (*Check to see that students are on the correct page.*)

Put your finger on the number 1. In this row there are a turtle, a lion, a giraffe, an elephant, and an ostrich. The animal I am thinking of has four feet. Which animal cannot be the one I am thinking of? (*the ostrich*) Cross it out.

Put your finger on the number 2. Now the ostrich is gone, and there are a turtle, a lion, a giraffe, and an elephant. The animal I am thinking of has a short neck. Which animal cannot be the one I am thinking of? (*the giraffe*) Cross it out. There are three animals left.

Put your finger on the number 3. Here are the three animals that are left. The animal I am thinking of does not have a shell. Which animal cannot be the one I am thinking of? (*the turtle*) Cross it out.

Put your finger on the number 4. There are two animals left. The animal I am thinking of has fur. Which animal cannot be the one I am thinking of? (*the elephant*) Cross it out.

So which animal is the most popular at the zoo? (*the lion*)

How did you figure out the animal I was thinking of? (*listened for clues; crossed out some animals*) The more wrong answers you can get rid of, the easier it is to guess the right answer. Remember to answer every question on a test. Sometimes you will have to guess. But first, get rid of the answers you know are not right. This will make you a good guesser.

Which Animal Is the Most Popular at the Zoo?

1.

○   ○   ○   ○   ○

2.

○   ○   ○   ○

3.

○   ○   ○

4.

○   ○

Try and Discuss

Read the script below to the children. This exercise introduces students to a sample test and gives the students a chance to discuss their answers.

Teacher Script

Now we have rows of four pictures again. We are going to practice getting rid of answers that cannot be right. This time the questions are hard. These questions are harder than the ones you will see on a real test. But I want you to get rid of two answers that cannot be right.

Put your finger on the number 1. An accountant is someone who works inside an office. Which one is a picture of an accountant? Look at the four pictures. Remember what you learned about guessing. Get rid of two answers that cannot be right. This time, do not cross them out. Guess which answer is right. Fill in the circle of your guess. (*Pause.*) Which one did you guess? (*doctor or <u>accountant</u>*) Why did you get rid of the other two? (*They show the persons working outside, and an accountant works inside.*) Remember to get rid of answers that cannot be right and then guess.

Put your finger on the number 2. This is the row I am going to ask you a question about. A whisk is very useful for making a cake. Which one is a whisk? Remember to get rid of two that cannot be right. (*Pause.*) Now guess and fill in the circle of your guess. Which one did you choose? (*the wire <u>whisk</u> or the scraper*) Why did you get rid of the other two? (*A screwdriver and a ball are not useful for making a cake.*) You are making good guesses now.

Put your finger on the number 3. This row has four numbers in it. Listen while I say the question. (*Pause.*) André is seven years old. His sister Tasha is two times older than André. How old is André's sister? Get rid of two answers that cannot be right. Fill in the circle of your guess. (*Pause.*) Which number did you guess? (*12 or <u>14</u>*) Why did you get rid of the other two? (*Because 5 and 2 are less than 7, and Tasha is older than André.*) Good guessing works for numbers or pictures.

Put your finger on the number 4. This question is about a house. Mr. Anderson's roof has a gable that's 14 feet high. Which picture shows Mr. Anderson's gable? (*Pause.*) Guess and fill in the circle. Which one did you guess? (*the chimney or <u>the gable</u>*) Why did you get rid of the other two? (*You couldn't see a roof at all.*)

Put your finger on the number 5. This is the last question. It is about shapes. Which picture shows a right triangle? (*Pause.*) Get rid of two. Make your guess and fill in the circle. (*Pause.*) Which one did you choose? (*the scalene or <u>right triangle</u>*) Why didn't you choose the other two? (*They are not triangles.*) Learning to be a good guesser is learning to get rid of answers that cannot be right.

ANSWER KEY

1. accountant (third picture) **2.** whisk (fourth picture) **3.** (14) **4.** the gable (first picture)
5. right triangle (fourth picture)

1.

○   ○   ○   ○

2.

○   ○   ○   ○

3. **14**   **12**   **5**   **2**

○   ○   ○   ○

4.

○   ○   ○   ○

5.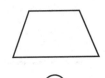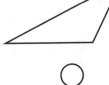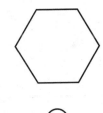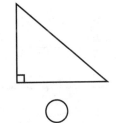

○   ○   ○   ○

Practice Test

Read the script below to the children. This sample test will help them practice guessing independently.

Teacher Script

Now that we have done some questions together and talked about them, it is time for you to try some on your own. I will ask a question about the pictures in each row. You will get rid of two answers. Then you will make a good guess and fill in the circle under it. We will not talk about your guesses until the end. You must listen quietly to the questions.

Put your finger on the number 1. This is the row of pictures I am going to ask you a question about. Listen to the question. A long time ago, people wrote with a quill pen. Which picture shows a quill pen? *(Pause.) (the fourth picture)* Mark your answer.

Put your finger on the number 2. Here is the next question. Jessica said, "Look! That fish sees its reflection in the mirror." Which picture shows a fish looking at its reflection? *(Pause.) (the second picture)* Make a good guess.

Put your finger on the number 3. Here is the question. Mr. Webb's umbrella protected him from the inclement weather. Which picture shows Mr. Webb protected by his umbrella from inclement weather? *(Pause.) (the third picture)*

Put your finger on the number 4. Here is the question. Mother said, "When you set the table, please make the plates and silverware symmetrical. That looks neater." Which picture shows the table set the way Mother wants it? *(Pause.) (the second picture)*

Put your finger on the number 5. Here is the question. Crustaceans are sea animals whose bodies are covered by hard shells. Which picture shows a crustacean? *(Pause.) (the third picture)*

Put your finger on the number 6. Here is the question. Which picture shows three parallel lines? *(Pause.) (the second picture)*

Do you see the stop sign at the bottom of the page? That means stop. Do not turn the page.

ANSWER KEY

1. quill pen (fourth picture) **2.** fish looking at a mirror (second picture) **3.** man with open umbrella in rainy weather (third picture) **4.** table with symmetrical setting (second picture) **5.** lobster (third picture) **6.** three parallel lines (second picture)

1.

  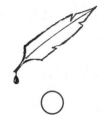

◯ ◯ ◯ ◯

2.

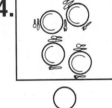 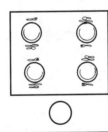  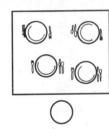

◯ ◯ ◯ ◯

3.

 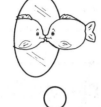 

◯ ◯ ◯ ◯

4.

◯ ◯ ◯ ◯

5.

  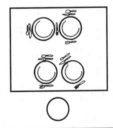 

◯ ◯ ◯ ◯

6.

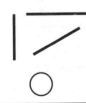 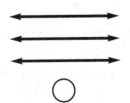 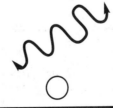 

◯ ◯ ◯ ◯

Language Arts: Phonemic Awareness

Phonemic awareness is the awareness of speech sounds. In first grade, the following skills are extremely important:

- blending the phonemes of one-syllable words.

- segmenting the phonemes of one-syllable words.

- counting the syllables in a word.

- changing beginning, middle, and end sounds to produce new words.

Teacher Script

Now it is time to practice choosing the right sounds of letters and of words. I will ask you questions about each row. You must listen carefully. I will not stop to discuss the answers, but I will go slowly enough for you. Remember to make good guesses like we have been practicing.

Put your finger on the number 1. Here is the question. Which picture begins with the same sound as "clock"? *(Pause.)* (*clown*)

Put your finger on the number 2. Here is the question. Which picture is the word I am sounding out now: "d...o...g"? *(Pause.)* (*dog*)

Put your finger on the number 3. You must listen carefully. Which picture rhymes with "dig"? *(Pause.)* (*pig*)

Put your finger on the number 4. Which picture is the word I am sounding out now: "b...a...t"? *(Pause.)* (*bat*)

Put your finger on the number 5. Listen carefully. Which word begins with the "sh" sound like in "show"? *(Pause.)* (*shoe*)

Put your finger on the number 6. This is the row we are on now. Here is the question. Which word rhymes with "sat"? *(Pause.)* (*mat*)

Turn the page.

1.

2.

3.

4.

5.

snowman	shoe	star	fish
○	○	○	○

6.

milk	man	mat	sun
○	○	○	○

Teacher Script *(cont.)*

Put your finger on the number 7. This is the row I am going to ask a question about now. Which picture begins with the same sound as "train"? *(Pause.)* *(truck)*

Put your finger on the number 8. Here is the question. Which word ends with the same sound as "hope"? *(Pause.)* *(rope)*

Put your finger on the number 9. Which picture rhymes with "house"? *(Pause.)* *(mouse)*

Put your finger on the number 10. This is a question about syllables or how many sound parts a word has. How many syllables are there in the word "table"? Fill in the circle under the number of your guess. The word is "table." *(Pause.)* *(2)*

Put your finger on the number 11. How many syllables or sound parts are there in the word "mother"? Fill in the circle under the number of your guess. The word is "mother." *(Pause.)* *(2)*

Put your finger on the number 12. Which word in the row has one syllable? *(Pause.)* *(house)*

Turn the page.

7.

◯   ◯   ◯   ◯

8.

| walk | sat | rope | roll |

◯   ◯   ◯   ◯

9.

◯   ◯   ◯   ◯

10.

1   **2**   **3**   **4**

◯   ◯   ◯   ◯

11.

1   **2**   **3**   **4**

◯   ◯   ◯   ◯

12.

| chicken | turtle | umbrella | house |

◯   ◯   ◯   ◯

Teacher Script *(cont.)*

Put your finger on the number 13. This is the row I am going to ask a question about. Which word has two syllables? *(Pause.)* *(lion)*

Put your finger on the number 14. *(Pause.)* If we change the "p" in "pig" to an "r," now which word is it? *(Pause.)* *(rig)*

Put your finger on the number 15. You must listen. *(Pause.)* If we change the "a" in "hat" to an "o," which word is it now? *(Pause.)* *(hot)*

Put your finger on the number 16. If we change the "m" in "make" to a "t" which word is it now? *(Pause.)* *(take)*

Put your finger on the number 17. If we change the "t" in "plate" to an "n," which word is it now? *(Pause.)* *(plane)*

Put your finger on the number 18. If we say "wheat" without the "wh" sound, which word is it now? *(Pause.)* *(eat)*

Now we stop.

ANSWER KEY

1. clown **2.** dog **3.** pig **4.** bat **5.** shoe **6.** mat **7.** truck **8.** rope **9.** mouse **10.** (2)
11. (2) **12.** house **13.** lion **14.** rig **15.** hot **16.** take **17.** plane **18.** eat

---

13.

bear	kite	ring	lion
○	○	○	○

14.

fig	dig	rig	rug
○	○	○	○

15.

hot	hit	hut	home
○	○	○	○

16.

cake	take	turn	snake
○	○	○	○

17.

plant	plot	plane	nut
○	○	○	○

18.

at	eat	feet	it
○	○	○	○

STOP

Language Arts: Decoding and Word Recognition

Decoding and word recognition are extremely important in reading. This language arts section includes the following:

- using sound-letter relationships to decode one-syllable words.
- recognizing common irregularly spelled words.
- using punctuation, syntax, and sentence and story meaning to decode one-syllable words.

Teacher Script

In this part of the test, you will answer questions about words. There is a sample at the top of your page.

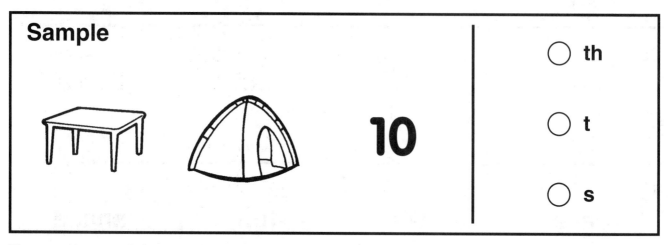

Here are pictures of three words that begin with the same letter. What letter do all these pictures begin with? Fill in the circle of your answer. *(Pause.)* They all begin with what letter? *(t)* That is right. Then you fill in the circle by the letter "t." Now you will answer some questions on your own.

Put your finger on the number 1. Look at the three pictures. All of pictures begin with the same letter. Which letter? Fill in the circle of your answer. *(Pause.)* *(b)*

Put your finger on the number 2. Look at the three pictures. All of the pictures begin with the same letter. Which letter? Fill in the circle of your answer. *(Pause.)* *(w)*

Put your finger on the number 3. Here is the question. These three pictures all begin with the same two letters. What are the two letters? *(Pause.)* *(tr)*

Put your finger on the number 4. These three pictures all have the same last two letters. What are they? *(Pause.)* *(ar)*

Put your finger on the number 5. Here is a word. Which word does it rhyme with? Fill in the circle of your answer. *(Pause.)* *(red)*

Put your finger on the number 6. Here is another word. Which word does it rhyme with? Fill in the circle of your answer. *(Pause.)* *(why)*

Turn the page.

Sample			10	○ th ○ t ○ s
1.				○ d ○ p ○ b
2.				○ v ○ w ○ h
3.				○ tw ○ tu ○ tr
4.				○ er ○ ar ○ ur
5.	**said**			○ feet ○ side ○ red
6.	**eye**			○ each ○ up ○ why

Teacher Script

Put your finger on the number 7. Here is one more word. What other word does it rhyme with? *(Pause.)* *(knees)*

Put your finger on the number 8. Now I am going to give you clues about a word. You listen to my clues, and you silently guess which word it is. I am thinking of a word. It is cold. It is white. You drink it. What am I thinking of? Fill in the circle of your answer. *(Pause.)* *(milk)*

Put your finger on the number 9. I am thinking of another word. You wear it. It fits tightly. It rhymes with "blue." What am I thinking of? Fill in the circle of your answer. *(Pause.)* *(shoe)*

Put your finger on the number 10. Listen to my little story. I had a sandwich for lunch. I drank some juice. I took a napkin and wiped off my _____. What did I wipe off? Fill in the circle of your guess. *(Pause.)* *(mouth)*

Put your finger on the number 11. Listen to another little story. I made supper. I made a pot of soup. I turned up the heat on the _____. What did I turn up the heat on? *(Pause.)* *(stove)*

Put your finger on the number 12. Here is my last little story. I flew my kite. I flew it high. It flew up with the _____. What did it fly up with? *(Pause.)* *(wind)*

Now stop.

ANSWER KEY
1. (b) **2.** (w) **3.** (tr) **4.** (ar) **5.** red **6.** why **7.** knees **8.** milk **9.** shoe **10.** mouth
11. stove **12.** wind

7.

please

- ○ police
- ○ knees
- ○ place

8.

snow	water	milk
○	○	○

9.

shoe	sock	hat
○	○	○

10.

smile	bag	mouth
○	○	○

11.

light	stove	match
○	○	○

12.

car	wind	rain
○	○	○

Language Arts: Spelling and Writing

In first grade, spelling and writing are crucial. This section includes the following skills:

- writing all the uppercase and lowercase letters of the alphabet.

- using phonics and patterns to spell three- and four-letter words.

- applying phonics to write independently.

- using basic punctuation and capitalization.

Teacher Script

Now it is time to practice capital letters, punctuation, and spelling. I will ask you questions about each row. You must listen carefully. I will not stop to discuss the answers, but I will go slowly enough for you. Remember to make good guesses like we have been practicing.

Put your finger on the number 1. This is the row we are on. Here is the question. Which letter is a capital letter? Fill in the circle of your answer. *(Pause.)* *(L)*

Put your finger on the number 2. Here is the question. Which letter is a lowercase letter? *(Pause.)* *(w)*

Put your finger on the number 3. Listen to what I say. I am going to say part of the alphabet. Which letter will come next? "Capital H, capital I, capital J, and capital—what letter comes next?" *(Pause.)* *(K)*

Put your finger on the number 4. Listen carefully. Which word should have a capital letter at the beginning? Fill in the circle of your answer. *(Pause.)* *(sara)*

Put your finger on the number 5. This time, read the four short sentences. Choose the sentence that is capitalized correctly. *(Pause.)* *(I am happy.)*

Put your finger on the number 6. Read the four short sentences. Choose the one that is punctuated correctly or has the correct end mark. Fill in the circle under your answer. *(Pause.)* *(What day is it?)*

Now stop.

ANSWER KEY

1. (L) **2.** (w) **3.** (K) **4.** sara **5.** I am happy. **6.** What day is it?

1.

m	p	L	a
○	○	○	○

2.

R	B	D	w
○	○	○	○

3.

L	K	I	M
○	○	○	○

4.

butter	sara	zoo	lunch
○	○	○	○

5.

i am happy.	i Am happy.	i am Happy.	I am happy.
○	○	○	○

6.

What day is it.	What day is it,	What day is it?	What day is it
○	○	○	○

STOP

Teacher Script

On this page, letters are missing in the words under the pictures. You must look at the picture, and you must decide what the word is for the picture. Then you must write the missing letters in the word. Here is a sample.

Sample

tra__ __   tr__ck   __ __unk

What missing letters would you write under the first picture? (*ck*) Yes, the word is "track." What missing letter would you write under the second picture? (*u*) Yes, because the word is "truck." And what missing letters would you write under the third picture? (*tr*) It is an elephant's trunk, isn't it? Remember—you look at the picture, decide what the word is, and write the missing letters under the picture.

Now, put your finger on the number 1. This is the row we are on. We will not discuss the answers now. Look at all three pictures. Think of the words. Write in the missing letters. Remember to always make a good guess. Answer every question. *(Pause.)* (<u>s</u>nowman, sn<u>ai</u>l, <u>s</u>nake)

Put your finger on the number 2. Look at the three pictures. Think of the words. Write in the missing letters. *(Pause.)* (<u>t</u>able, <u>a</u>pple, <u>pe</u>ople)

Put your finger on the number 3. This is the row we are on now. Look at the pictures. Think. Write in the missing letters. *(Pause.)* (pa<u>n</u>, <u>m</u>an, f<u>a</u>n)

Put your finger on the number 4. Look at the pictures. Think. Write in the missing letters. *(Pause.)* (co<u>at</u>, <u>g</u>host, toa<u>st</u>)

Put your finger on the number 5. Look at the pictures. Write in the missing letters. *(Pause.)* (ri<u>ng</u>, <u>sw</u>ing, <u>w</u>ing)

Put your finger on the number 6. Look at the pictures. Write in the missing letters. *(Pause.)* (bo<u>at</u>, n<u>ote</u>, <u>g</u>oat)

Now stop.

ANSWER KEY

1. <u>s</u>nowman, sn<u>ai</u>l, <u>s</u>nake **2.** <u>t</u>able, <u>a</u>pple, <u>pe</u>ople **3.** pa<u>n</u>, <u>m</u>an, f<u>a</u>n **4.** co<u>at</u>, <u>g</u>host, toa<u>st</u> **5.** ri<u>ng</u>, <u>sw</u>ing, <u>w</u>ing **6.** bo<u>at</u>, n<u>ote</u>, <u>g</u>oat

---

Language Arts: Spelling and Writing *(cont.)*

Sample

tra___ ___   tr___ck   ___ ___unk

1.

___ ___owman   sn___ ___l   s___ ___ke

2.

___ ___ble   ___ ___ple   ___ ___ople

3.

pa___   ___an   f___n

4.

co___ ___   ___ ___ost   toa___ ___

5.

ri___ ___   ___ ___ing   ___ng

6.

bo___ ___   n___ ___e   ___ ___at

Language Arts: Language, Comprehension, and Response

In this section, language and comprehension skills for first grade include the following:

- reading and comprehending narrative and expository text.
- elaborating on how information and events connect to life experiences.
- predicting and explaining what will happen next in stories.
- understanding the concept of a sentence.
- responding to what, when, where, and how questions.

Teacher Script

In this section, you will read silently on your own. You will find that a word is missing. You will choose which word is missing. At the top of the page is a sample. This is a chance to practice the kind of work you will be doing on this page. Let's do the sample together. (*Check to see that students are on the correct page.*)

Put your finger on the first sentence in the sample box. Now read the all sentences silently to yourself.

Sample

I have a pet. My pet will bark, run, and jump. My pet is a

_____.

   ○   ○   ○   ○

  cat   bird   dog   fish

Fill in the circle under the answer you choose. (*Pause.*) Which one did you choose? (*dog*)

Now you will read more sentences like these on your own. There will be a word missing. You choose the missing word and fill in the circle under it. We will not discuss each answer. Remember to stop when you see the stop sign at the bottom of the page. (*Pause for questions.*)

Put your finger on the number 1. This is the first question. Read silently. Fill in the circle of your answer. (*Pause.*) (*hat*)

Put your finger on the number 2. This is where you should be. Read silently. Fill in the circle of your answer. (*Pause.*) (*water*)

Put your finger on the number 3. Read silently. Fill in the circle of your answer. (*Pause.*) (*slept*)

Put your finger on the number 4. This is where you should be. Read silently. Fill in the circle of your answer. (*Pause.*) (*party*)

Put your finger on the number 5. Fill in the circle of your answer. (*Pause.*) (*bike*)

Turn the page.

Language Arts: Language, Comprehension, and Response *(cont.)*

Sample

I have a pet. My pet will bark, and run, and jump. My pet is a _____.

○ cat   ○ bird   ○ dog   ○ fish

---

1. The wind was strong. It blew hard. It blew dad's _____ off.

○ ring   ○ car   ○ sock   ○ hat

---

2. Mother said, "Stay on the beach. Don't go in the _____."

○ sand   ○ water   ○ shell   ○ umbrella

---

3. The kitten was tired. It _____ all day.

○ cooked   ○ read   ○ flew   ○ slept

---

4. We had a _____. We had ice cream, cake, and gifts.

○ bath   ○ fire   ○ party   ○ music

---

5. My _____ had a flat tire. I could not ride in the parade.

○ bike   ○ balloon   ○ boat   ○ bag

Teacher Script *(cont.)*

Put your finger on the number 6. Read the sentence. Fill in the circle of your answer. *(Pause.)* *(day)*

Put your finger on the number 7. This is the row. Read silently. *(Pause.)* *(run)*

Now put your finger on the number 8. That is right. Read silently. *(Pause.)* *(sister)*

Put your finger on the number 9. This is the row you should be on now. Fill in the circle of your answer. *(Pause.)* *(cat)*

Put your finger on the number 10. Read silently and fill in the circle of your answer. *(Pause.)* *(clock)*

Put your finger on the number 11. This is the last row. Read carefully. *(Pause.)* *(floor)*

Now stop.

ANSWER KEY

1. hat **2.** water **3.** slept **4.** party **5.** bike **6.** day **7.** run **8.** sister **9.** cat **10.** clock **11.** floor

---

6. I sleep at night. I don't sleep in the _____.

○ time   ○ day   ○ bed   ○ night

7. I know how to hop. I know how to skip. I know how to

_____.

○ run   ○ say   ○ paint   ○ talk

8. There is a girl in my family. I am her brother. She is my

_____.

○ friend   ○ mother   ○ sister   ○ teacher

9. It goes meow! It has fur. It is a _____.

○ cow   ○ pillow   ○ cat   ○ fish

10. Tick tock, tick tock says the _____.

○ box   ○ clock   ○ time   ○ sun

11. There was no chair. I sat on the _____.

○ dog   ○ water   ○ floor   ○ light

Language Arts: Language, Comprehension, and Response *(cont.)*

Teacher Script

Are you ready? (*Check to make sure students are on the correct page.*) Now I am going to read you a story. It is about someone named Arlo. Arlo orders gardening tools by mail. How does it work when you order something by mail? (*discussion*) Have you ever sent away for something by mail? (*discussion*) Do you expect to get what you ordered? (*discussion*) What if you get the wrong thing sent to you? (*discussion*) You'll see what Arlo did.

I will stop during the story and ask you questions. We will not talk about the answers. You will fill in the circle of your answer. Listen carefully to the story and the questions I will ask. (*Begin the story, stopping at the breaks to ask students the questions.*)

Arlo Orders by Mail

Arlo lived in a house with trees in the yard. The air was turning cold.

"Summer is over," he said. "The leaves will be falling soon."

When he got his mail the next day, there was a postcard.

It said, "Get ready for fall! Order a shovel and rake now."

"Shovel and rake?" said Arlo. "Great, I need a shovel and rake for fall."

So he called the phone number on the card and ordered a shovel and rake.

The next day, he got a box in the mail.

It said, "To Arlo: Cups and plates."

"Cups and plates? I ordered a shovel and rake."

He called the phone number on the card and said, "Please send me a shovel and rake, not cups and plates."

Put your finger on the number 1. This is the row for the question I am going to ask. Here it is. What did Arlo order by mail? Fill in the circle of your answer. (*Pause.*) (*shovel and rake*) Now here is more of the story.

The next day, the box of cups and plates was gone.

There was a new box outside Arlo's door.

Teacher Script *(cont.)*

He opened it.

"Who are you?" Arlo said.

"Friendly snake."

"Friendly snake? I ordered a shovel and rake."

"Shovel and rake?" said the snake. "Not cups and plates?"

"No."

"Not a friendly snake?"

"No."

"Sorry, our mistake."

Arlo called the phone number. "No friendly snake, no cups and plates, just a shovel and snake—I mean, a shovel and rake! That's all. And hurry, the leaves are turning gold."

Put your finger on the number 2. Here is the question. What time of year is it in the story? Fill in the circle of your answer. *(Pause.)* *(leaves falling)* Now, here is more of the story.

The next day the box with the friendly snake was gone.

There was a new box.

It said, "To Arlo: Instant lake. Just add water."

"Instant lake? Instant lake?" said Arlo. "This isn't what I ordered. I ordered a shovel and rake."

Put your finger on the number 3. Here is the question. What do you think Arlo will do next? Fill in the circle of your answer. *(Pause.)* *(man telephoning)*

He called the phone number. "No instant lake, cups and plates, friendly snake. I need a shovel and rake!"

The next day, the box of instant lake was gone.

There was a new box.

It said, "To Arlo: Mix-and-bake chocolate cake."

Teacher Script (cont.)

"I can't wait," Arlo said. "I can't wait any longer for a shovel and rake. It's getting too late. The leaves are falling."

He called the phone number. "You have sent me cups and plates, a friendly snake, an instant lake, a mix-and-bake chocolate cake. I need a shovel and rake!"

"Airplane brake?"

"No, a shovel and rake."

"Dates in a crate?"

"No, no!"

Put your finger on the number 4. What is another word that would rhyme with "brake and "rake"? Fill in the circle of your answer. *(Pause.)* *(shake)*

"Spell what you want, please," said the person on the phone to Arlo.
Arlo spelled what he wanted. "S-H-O-V-E-L A-N-D R-A-K-E."

"Got it, great."

"And hurry," said Arlo. "It's getting so late."

The next day, the box of mix-and-bake chocolate cake was gone.

There was a new box.

Put your finger on the number 5. What do you think will be in the box this time? Fill in the circle of your answer. *(Pause.)* *(shovel and rake)*

The new box said, "To Arlo: Shovel and rake. Sorry, our mistake."

Arlo took out the shovel and rake. They were just what he needed.

He raked the leaves. He used the shovel in his garden.

Then he jumped in a great big pile of leaves.

"A shovel and rake, just what I needed, and not too late," he said.

The End

Put your finger on the number 6. Here is the question. Why did Arlo get what he wanted at last? Fill in the circle of your answer. *(Pause.)* *(He spelled the words.)*

Now stop.

ANSWER KEY

1. shovel and rake **2.** leaves falling **3.** man telephoning **4.** shake **5.** shovel and rake
6. He spelled the words.

1. ○ ○ ○ ○

2. ○ ○ ○ ○

3. ○ ○ ○ ○

4.

rain   shake   wood   stamp

○ ○ ○ ○

5. ○ ○ ○ ○

6.

He cried.   He did nothing.   He went home.   He spelled the words.

○ ○ ○ ○

STOP

The first grade math skills in this section include the following:

- counting using one-to-one correspondence.
- comparing/sequencing numerals.
- making sets; matching numerals.
- identifying ordinal position.
- reading and writing numerals 1–10.
- rote counting by ones, twos, fives, and tens.
- recognizing one more/less, before/after/between.
- grouping objects into tens and ones.
- making reasonable estimates.
- representing numbers in a variety of ways.
- solving problems using addition and subtraction.
- using counting strategies to find sums/differences.

Teacher Script

Now I am going to ask questions about numbers and counting. I will ask you a question. You will look at the choices and then fill in the circle of your answer. Let's do a sample question first.

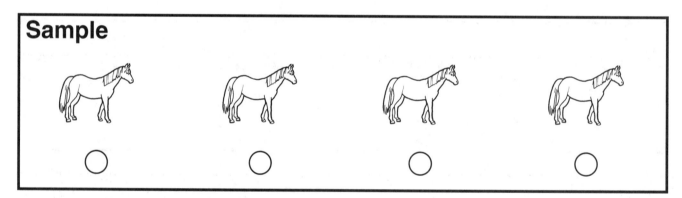

Sample

Look at the four horses standing in a line. (*Make sure students are in the correct place.*) Fill in the circle of the horse that is third in line. (*Pause.*) Which one is third? (*Illustrate on the board.*) Now you will answer some questions on your own. We will not discuss them.

Put your finger on the number 1. Here is the question. Which number comes between 7 and 9? (*Pause.*) (*8*)

Put your finger on the number 2. Which number would be next: 4, 6, 8, ___. (*Pause.*) (*10*)

Put your finger on the number 3. Which number comes before 13? (*Pause.*) (*12*)

Put your finger on the number 4. Which number is less than 7? (*Pause.*) (*6*)

Put your finger on the number 5. Look at the pictures of blocks. The tall stacks of blocks have 10 each. The short stacks have five each. How many blocks are in the picture? (*Pause.*) (*30*)

Put your finger on the number 6. Look at the stacks of blocks. Which stack has 25 blocks? (*Pause.*) (*the second one*)

Turn the page.

Sample

○	○	○	○

1.

6	**8**	**10**	**11**
○	○	○	○

2.

2	**12**	**10**	**14**
○	○	○	○

3.

14	**15**	**16**	**12**
○	○	○	○

4.

8	**9**	**6**	**7**
○	○	○	○

5.

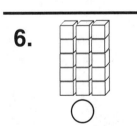 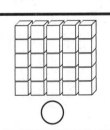 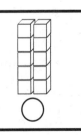 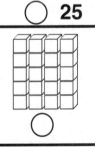

○ 15
○ 4
○ 30
○ 25

6.

○	○	○	○

Teacher Script *(cont.)*

Put your finger on the number 7. Look at the picture of the cupcakes. How many cupcakes are there in all? Write the number on the line. *(Pause.)* *(5)*

Put your finger on the number 8. Look at the picture of the birds. How many birds are there in all? Write the number on the line. *(Pause.)* *(7)*

Put your finger on the number 9. Look at the picture of the blocks. How many blocks are there in all? Write the number on the line. *(Pause.)* *(6)*

Put your finger on the number 10. Look at the picture of circles and triangles. How many shapes are there in all? Write the number on the line. *(Pause.)* *(6)*

Put your finger on the number 11. Look at the picture of the animals. How many animals are there in all? Write the number on the line. *(Pause.)* *(5)*

Put your finger on the number 12. Look at the picture of the stars. How many stars are there in all? Write the number on the line. *(Pause.)* *(9)*

Now stop.

ANSWER KEY

1. (8) **2.** (10) **3.** (12) **4.** (6) **5.** (30) **6.** 25 blocks (second picture) **7.** (5) **8.** (7) **9.** (6)

10. (6) **11.** (5) **12.** (9)

7.

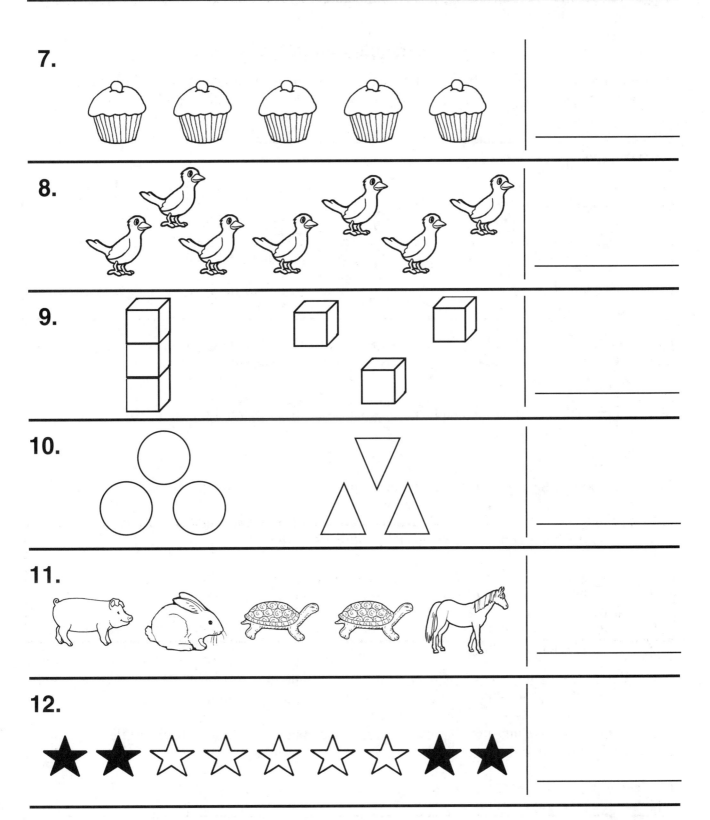

8.

9.

10.

11.

12.

Teacher Script

Now we are going to make guesses about numbers. The choices are in rows again. I will ask a question, and you will fill in the circle of your answer. First, let's do addition problems. Here is a sample.

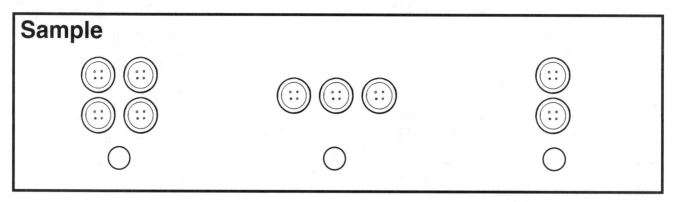

Sample

Kim had two buttons on her dress. Her mother sewed on two more buttons. How many buttons are on Kim's dress now? Fill in the circle of your answer. *(Pause.)* *(four buttons)* *(Draw on the board to illustrate the problem.)*

Now you will answer the addition problems on your own. Listen carefully while I ask each question. We will not discuss the answers.

Put your finger on the number 1. This is the row we are on. Three cars drove into the parking lot. Then three more came. How many cars are in the parking lot now? *(Pause.)* *(six cars)*

Put your finger on the number 2. Mrs. Carter had ten small plants for her garden. Then she bought two more. How many plants does she have in all? *(Pause.)* *(twelve plants)*

Put your finger on the number 3. Two ants crawled out of an anthill. Two more ants crawled out to join them. How many ants crawled out of the hill in all? *(Pause.)* *(four ants)*

Put your finger on the number 4. There were three eggs in a nest. The mother bird laid two more. How many eggs are in the nest? *(Pause.)* *(five eggs)*

Put your finger on the number 5. There were two fish swimming in one bowl and three fish swimming in another bowl. How many fish are swimming in all? *(Pause.)* *(five fish)*

Put your finger on the number 6. One butterfly was on a branch. Two more butterflies flew nearby. How many butterflies were there in all? *(Pause.)* *(three butterflies)*

Now stop.

ANSWER KEY

1. six cars **2.** twelve plants **3.** four ants **4.** five eggs **5.** five fish **6.** three butterflies

---

Mathematics: Whole Numbers (cont.)

Sample

1.

⭘   ⭘   ⭘   ⭘

2.

⭘   ⭘   ⭘   ⭘

3.

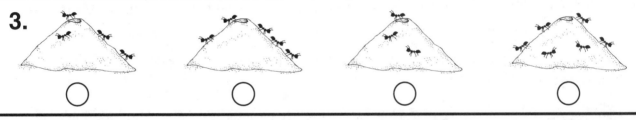

⭘   ⭘   ⭘   ⭘

4.

⭘   ⭘   ⭘   ⭘

5.

⭘   ⭘   ⭘   ⭘

6.

⭘   ⭘   ⭘   ⭘

STOP

Teacher Script

This time we will do subtraction or take-away problems. This part of the test is different from the addition part. The answers will be numbers, not pictures. Here is a sample.

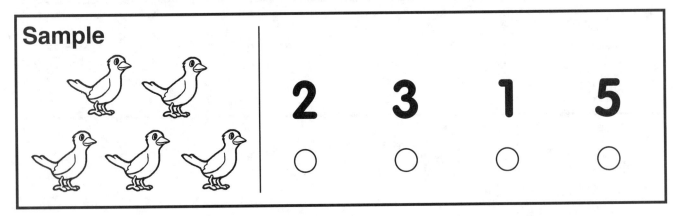

Sample 2 3 1 5

Look at the birds. There were five birds on the ground. Two of the birds flew away. How many birds are left on the ground? Fill in the circle under the number that shows how many birds are left on the ground. *(Pause.)* How many birds were left? *(three)*

Now you will answer questions on your own. Remember, this time the questions are about subtraction or taking away.

Put your finger on the number 1. Mario has five pears. He gave three pears to Audrey. How many pears did Mario have left? Fill in the circle under your answer. *(Pause.)* *(2)*

Put your finger on the number 2. Todd gave his dog, Dilly, six dog biscuits. Dilly ate two of them right away. How many biscuits did Dilly have left? *(Pause.)* *(4)*

Put your finger on the number 3. Jason had seven cookies in his lunch. If he gave four cookies to his friend, how many cookies would Jason have left? Fill in the circle of your answer. *(Pause.)* *(3)*

Put your finger on the number 4. Four children were playing in the yard. Two of them went home for lunch. How many children stayed to play in the yard. *(Pause.)* *(2)*

Put your finger on the number 5. Howard had three books. He returned one to the library. How many books does Howard have left? *(Pause.)* *(2)*

Put your finger on the number 6. Lisa had ten blocks. She stacked up seven of them. How many blocks did Lisa not use in her stack? *(Pause.)* *(3)*

Now stop.

ANSWER KEY

1. (2) **2.** (4) **3.** (3) **4.** (2) **5.** (2) **6.** (3)

Mathematics: Whole Numbers (cont.)

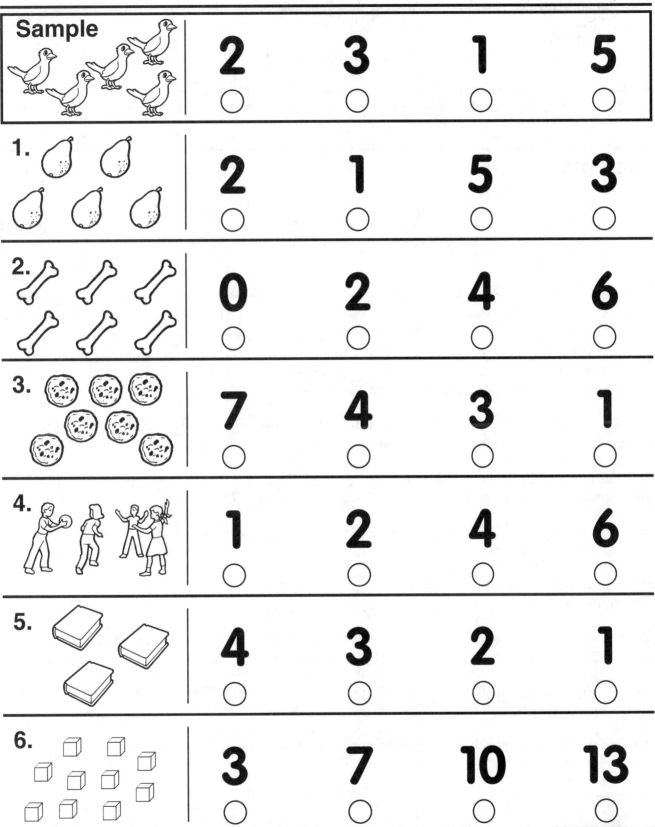

Sample

2 ○   3 ○   1 ○   5 ○

1.

2 ○   1 ○   5 ○   3 ○

2.

0 ○   2 ○   4 ○   6 ○

3.

7 ○   4 ○   3 ○   1 ○

4.

1 ○   2 ○   4 ○   6 ○

5.

4 ○   3 ○   2 ○   1 ○

6.

3 ○   7 ○   10 ○   13 ○

STOP

Teacher Script

In this part of the test, you will choose pairs of numbers that go together. What is a "pair"? (*discussion*) Here is a sample of the kinds of questions we will be answering. (*Check to make sure students are on the correct page.*)

Sample				
2, 4	3, 5	4, 6	5, _	○ 4 ○ 3 ○ 7

Look at these pairs of numbers. They go together in a special way. How do they go together? (*In each pair, the second number is two more than the first.*) How the numbers go together is their pattern. Look at the pattern. (*Repeat the pairs.*) What should be the number with 5 in the last pair? Fill in the circle of your answer. (*Pause.*) What should be the number with 5 in the last pair? (*7*) Why? (*Because it is two more than 5 like the rest of the pattern.*)

Now you will answer some questions about patterns of numbers on your own. We will not stop to discuss them. (*Make sure students have adequate time to identify patterns.*)

Put your finger on the number 1. Listen to my question. Look at the pairs of numbers. What is the missing number in the pattern? Fill in the circle of your answer. (*Pause.*) (*3*)

Put your finger on the number 2. Look at the pairs of numbers. What is the missing number in the pattern? (*Pause.*) (*4*)

Put your finger on the number 3. Look at the pairs of numbers. What is the missing number in the pattern? (*Pause.*) (*5*)

Put your finger on the number 4. Look at the pictures of black dots. They are in pairs like numbers. What is the missing number of black dots? (*Pause.*) (*three dots*)

Put your finger on the number 5. Look at the pictures of black dots. They are in pairs again. What is the missing number of black dots? (*Pause.*) (*two dots*)

Put your finger on the number 6. Now numbers and black dots are in pairs. What is the missing number? (*Pause.*) (*4*)

Now stop.

ANSWER KEY

1. (3) **2.** (4) **3.** (5) **4.** three dots **5.** two dots **6.** (4)

Sample

2, 4   3, 5   4, 6   5, _

- ○ 4
- ○ 3
- ○ 7

1.

2, 1   2, 2   2, _   2, 4

- ○ 2
- ○ 3
- ○ 4

2.

1, 2   2, 4   _, 8   8, 16

- ○ 4
- ○ 8
- ○ 6

3.

1, 3   5, 7   3, 1   7, _

- ○ 5
- ○ 3
- ○ 7

4.

- ○
- ○
- ○

5.

- ○
- ○
- ○

6.

1, ⚁   2, ⚂   3, ⚃   _ , ⚄

- ○ 7
- ○ 5
- ○ 4

STOP

Mathematics: Geometric Ideas

This first grade math skills section includes the following:

- identifying plane and solid figures in the environment.
- using directional and positional words.
- identifying likenesses and differences.

Teacher Script

Now we are going to talk about shapes. The questions in this part of the test will show you shapes. You will make guesses. Here is a sample.

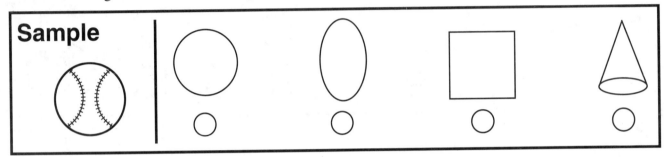

Here is a picture of a baseball. Look at its shape. Now look at the row of shapes next to the baseball. What shape does the baseball look like? Fill in the circle of your answer. *(Pause.)* What shape is the baseball like? *(a circle)* Now you will answer more questions on your own. Listen carefully.

Put your finger on the number 1. Look at the suitcase. Which word describes the shape of the suitcase? Fill in the circle under your answer. *(Pause.) (rectangle)*

Put your finger on the number 2. Look at the picture of the plate, the clock and the ball. Which group of shapes do they belong with? *(Pause.) (circles, the third group)*

Put your finger on the number 3. Look at the picture of the book, the mat, and board game. Which group of shapes do they belong with? *(Pause.) (rectangles, the first group)*

Put your finger on the number 4. Look at the pictures. Which picture shows the coffee cup to the left of the table? *(Pause.) (the second one)*

Put your finger on the number 5. Look at the pictures of the animals. Which animal is doing something different? *(Pause.) (the frog beside the rock)*

Put your finger on the number 6. Look at the picture of the square that is half black and half white. Which other square has the same amount of black and white? *(Pause.) (the second picture)*

Now stop.

ANSWER KEY

1. rectangle **2.** circles **3.** rectangles **4.** coffee cup to the left of the table (the second picture) **5.** the frog beside the rock (the third picture) **6.** the second picture

---

Mathematics: Geometric Ideas (cont.)

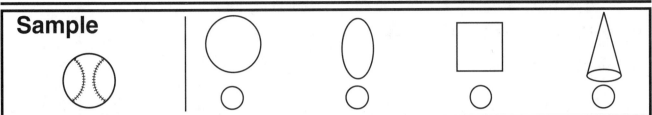

Sample

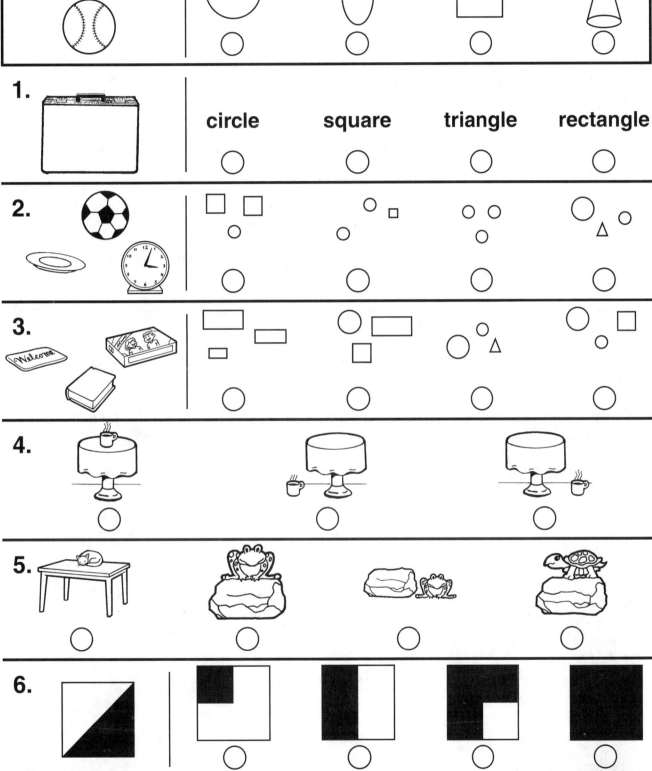

1.

  circle square triangle rectangle

2.

3.

4.

5.

6.

Mathematics: Classification and Pattern

This first grade math skills section includes the following:

- sorting by attribute.

- continuing patterns.

- finding and correcting errors in patterns.

- identifying patterns in the environment.

Teacher Script

Put your finger on the number 1. Look at the triangle by itself. Which group of shapes does it belong with? Fill in the circle under your answer. *(Pause.)* (*set of triangles*)

Put your finger on the number 2. Look at the rectangle by itself. A rectangle has four sides. Which shape does it belong with? *(Pause.)* (*trapezoid*)

Put your finger on the number 3. Look at the pattern of things to eat. Which thing to eat should come next? Fill in the circle under the picture. *(Pause.)* (*apple*)

Put your finger on the number 4. Look at the pattern of animals in a row. One animal is not in the right place. Which one? *(Pause.)* (*cat*)

Put your finger on the number 5. Look at the groups of flowers. Which group of flowers is different from the rest? Fill in the circle under the one that does not belong. *(Pause.)* (*fourth picture with rose*)

Put your finger on the number 6. Look at the four pictures. One does not belong with the others. Which one? *(Pause.)* (*ice-cream cone*)

Turn the page.

Mathematics: Classification and Pattern *(cont.)*

1.

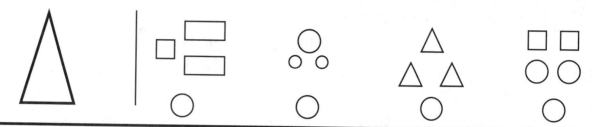

2.

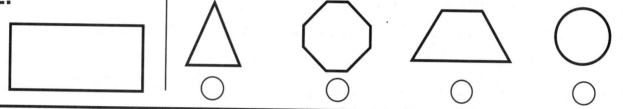

3.

4.

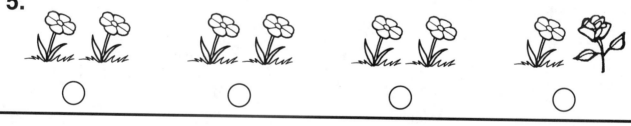

5.

6.

Teacher Script (cont.)

Put your finger on the number 7. Look at the pictures. You see these things in the world. Which one has a pattern? *(Pause.)* *(railroad tracks)*

Put your finger on the number 8. Here is a picture of the pyramids in Egypt. If another one was going to be built, what shape would it have? Fill in the circle under your answer. *(Pause.)* *(triangle)*

Put your finger on the number 9. Here is a picture of the back of an envelope. What four shapes do the lines make? *(Pause.)* *(four triangles)*

Put your finger on the number 10. Which of these has a pattern? Fill in the circle of your answer. *(Pause.)* *(soccer ball)*

Put your finger on the number 11. One of these pictures does not belong. Which one? *(Pause.)* *(coin)*

Put your finger on the number 12. One of these pictures does not belong. Which one? *(Pause.)* *(carrot)*

Now stop.

ANSWER KEY

1. set of triangles **2.** trapezoid **3.** apple **4.** cat **5.** fourth picture with rose **6.** ice-cream cone **7.** railroad tracks **8.** triangle **9.** four triangles **10.** soccer ball **11.** coin **12.** carrot

---

7.

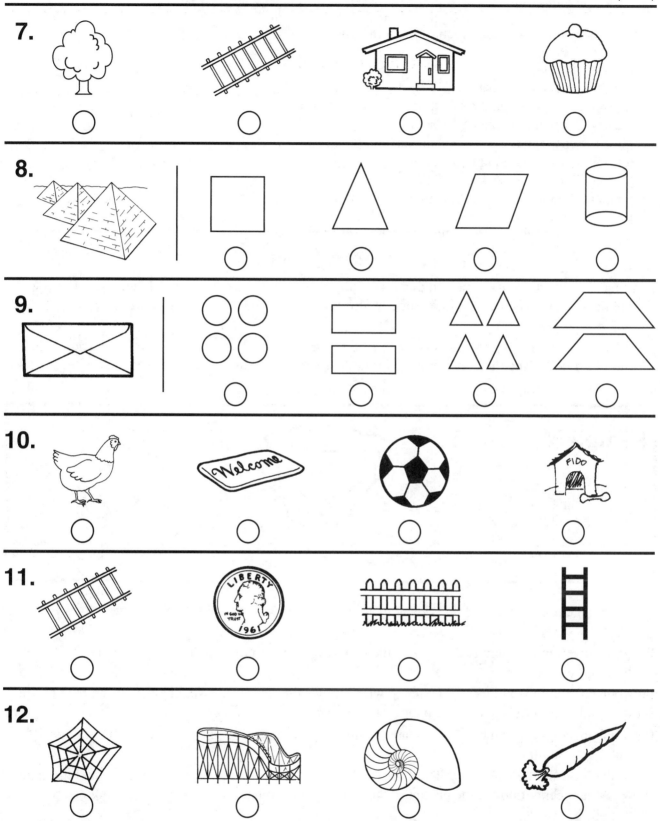

8.

9.

10.

11.

12.

The math skills in this section include the following:

- comparing objects.
- identifying unequal parts.
- naming and ordering days of the week, months of the year.
- using information on a calendar.
- identifying values of a penny, nickel, and dime.
- using non-standard units to measure.
- using time-related words.
- telling time to the the nearest hour.

Teacher Script

It is time we talked about—time! In this part of the book we answer questions about time. There will be questions about time on the clock, about which comes first and second, and about the days of the week.

There will also be measuring questions in this part of the book. Here is a sample of a question about measuring. Look at the three measuring cups at the top of your page. Which one holds the most? (*the largest measuring cup*)

Sample

Put your finger on the number 1. Look at the pictures about baking a cake. Which one comes first? (*Pause.*) (*the eggs, milk, and flour*)

Put your finger on the number 2. Look at the pictures about painting. Which happened last? (*Pause.*) (*completed clown face*)

Put your finger on the number 3. Listen to what a boy said. He said, "We laughed during the puppet show." Which picture is during the puppet show? (*Pause.*) (*the first picture*)

Put your finger on the number 4. Here are pictures of four clocks. Which one shows the time of 10 o'clock? (*Pause.*) (*the first clock*)

Put your finger on the number 5. There are two kinds of clocks: those with round faces, and those that show just numbers. Look at the picture of the round clock. What time is it showing in numbers? (*Pause.*) (*3:30*)

Put your finger on the number 6. Here is a little story. Two girls were selling lemonade on a hot day. "Five cents! Five cents!" they called. A thirsty runner stopped and said, "I have a nickel." "OK," they said. And they gave him a glass of lemonade. Which coin is a nickel? (*Pause.*) (*the fourth coin*)

Now turn the page.

Sample

○   ○   ○

1.

○   ○   ○   ○

2.

○   ○   ○   ○

3.

○   ○   ○   ○

4.

○   ○   ○   ○

5.

| 2:30 | 4:30 | 3:30 | 3:45 |

○   ○   ○   ○

6.

○   ○   ○   ○

Teacher Script (cont.)

Put your finger on the number 7. A boy named Marcus bought two pieces of gum with a dime. Which coin is a dime? *(Pause.)* *(second coin)*

Put your finger on the number 8. Now let's talk about months and days. Here are some of the months of the year in order. But which month is missing? Fill in the circle of your choice. *(Pause.)* *(August)*

Put your finger on the number 9. Here is the question. Listen carefully. What month comes after October? *(Pause.)* *(November)*

Put your finger on the number 10. Here are some of the days of the week in order. One is missing. Which one? *(Pause.)* *(Thursday)*

Put your finger on the number 11. Here is the question. Listen carefully. What are the days of the weekend? *(Pause.)* *(Saturday/Sunday)*

Put your finger on the number 12. Listen to the question. How many days are in a week? *(Pause.)* *(7)*

Now stop.

ANSWER KEY

1. eggs, milk, and flour **2.** completed clown face **3.** the first picture **4.** the first clock **5.** (3:30)
6. the fourth coin **7.** second coin **8.** August **9.** November **10.** Thursday **11.** Saturday/Sunday
12. (7)

7.

◯   ◯   ◯   ◯

8.

June, July, _____, September, October

◯ May
◯ August
◯ March
◯ December

9.

December   September   November   January

◯   ◯   ◯   ◯

10.

Tuesday, Wednesday, _____, Friday

◯ Thursday
◯ Monday
◯ Saturday
◯ Sunday

11.
Monday
Tuesday

Thursday
Friday

Saturday
Sunday

Sunday
Monday

◯   ◯   ◯   ◯

12.

5   **6**   **7**   **4**

◯   ◯   ◯   ◯

Teacher Script

This is a calendar for one month of the year. I am going to ask you some questions about the calendar.

March						
Sun.	Mon.	Tues.	Wed.	Thurs.	Fri.	Sat.
	1	2	3	4	5	6
7	8	9	10	11	12	13
14	15	16	17	18	19	20
21	22	23	24	25	26	27
28	29	30	31			

Put your finger on the number 1. Which month is this calendar for? *(Pause.)* *(March)*

Put your finger on the number 2. On which day of the week does this month begin? *(Pause.)* *(Mon.)*

Put your finger on the number 3. Which day of the month is the 12th on? *(Pause.)* *(Fri.)*

Put your finger on the number 4. How many days does this month have? *(Pause.)* *(31)*

Turn the page.

March						
Sun.	Mon.	Tues.	Wed.	Thurs.	Fri.	Sat.
	1	2	3	4	5	6
7	8	9	10	11	12	13
14	15	16	17	18	19	20
21	22	23	24	25	26	27
28	29	30	31			

1.

Mon.	March	Fri.	Sat.
○	○	○	○

2.

Sun.	Sat.	Wed.	Mon.
○	○	○	○

3.

Wed.	Thurs.	Fri.	Sat.
○	○	○	○

4.

28	29	30	31
○	○	○	○

Teacher Script *(cont.)*

Now we will answer more questions about measuring.

Put your finger on the number 5. Look at the black lines. Which one is half as long as the other? *(Pause.)* *(the fourth set of lines)*

Put your finger on the number 6. Look at the three pictures. Which would be the longest trip? *(Pause.)* *(the river)*

Put your finger on the number 7. Look at the pictures of the animals. Which is the heaviest animal? *(Pause.)* *(the horse)*

Put your finger on the number 8. Look at the pictures. Which thing is the most expensive? *(Pause.)* *(the computer)*

Put your finger on the number 9. Listen to my question. Which is the smallest? *(Pause.)* *(wristwatch)*

Put your finger on the number 10. Look at the pictures. Which one is the lightest? *(Pause.)* *(the feather)*

Now stop.

ANSWER KEY

1. March **2.** Mon. **3.** Fri. **4.** (31) **5.** fourth set of lines **6.** river **7.** horse **8.** computer
9. wristwatch **10.** feather

5.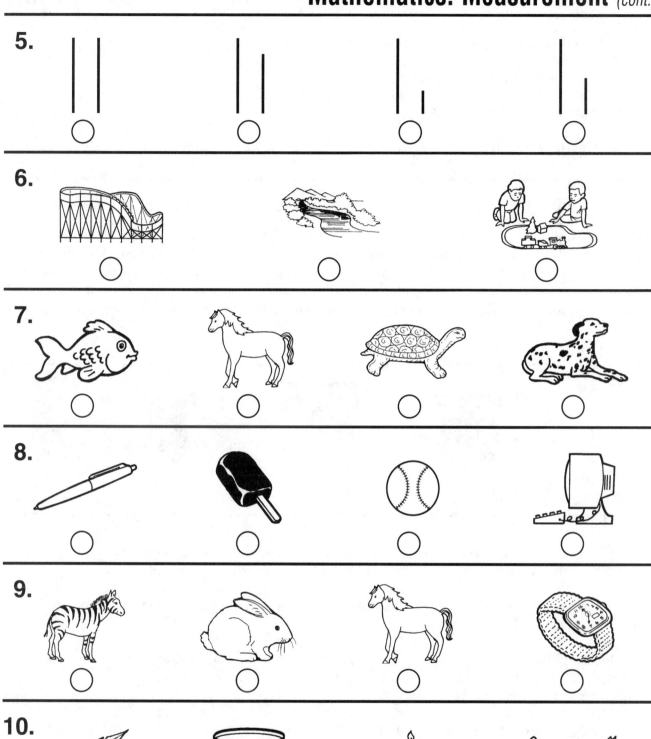

6.

7.

8.

9.

10.

Mathematics: Problem Solving

The math skills in this section include the following:

- solving spatial visualization puzzles.

- estimating reasonable solutions.

- copying simple designs.

Teacher Script

Do you know what a puzzle is? What is a puzzle? (*discussion*) What makes a puzzle fun to do? (*discussion*) In this part of the book, you will be answering questions that are like puzzles. Here is a sample at the top of your page. Here is a triangle. Look at the row of four black shapes next to it. Which shape is like the triangle? Fill in the circle of your answer. (*Pause.*) Which one did you choose? (*upside-down triangle*) Why? (*discussion*) Now you will do some of these puzzles on your own. Listen carefully.

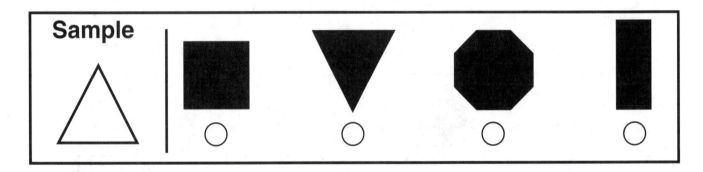

Put your finger on the number 1. Look at the pictures. If these things were in alphabetical order, which one would be first? Fill in the circle under your answer. (*Pause.*) (*the balloon*)

Put your finger on the number 2. Look at the pictures. Now, if these pictures were in alphabetical order, which one would be last? (*Pause.*) (*the zebra*)

Put your finger on the number 3. Listen to my question. There are three pictures this time. If they were in alphabetical order, which one would be in the middle? (*Pause.*) (*dress*)   .

Put your finger on the number 4. Look at the picture of the strange shape that looks like a C. Which one of the other shapes looks like it? Fill in the circle under your answer. (*Pause.*) (*the fourth shape*)

Put your finger on the number 5. Look at the four shapes. Pretend they are being cut where the dotted lines are. If you cut them on the dotted lines, which one will make two triangles? (*Pause.*) (*the fourth picture*)

Put your finger on the number 6. Here is another question about cutting. Look at the four pictures. If you cut the shapes on the dotted lines, which one will make two equal parts? (*Pause.*) (*the square*)

Turn the page.

Sample

1.

2.

3.

4.

5.

6.

Mathematics: Problem Solving (cont.)

Teacher Script (cont.)

Put your finger on the number 7. Look at the picture of the scissors cutting a piece of paper. What shape will the scissors cut out? *(Pause.)* *(the triangle)*

Put your finger on the number 8. Look at the picture of the box. Which is the only other box that will fit inside it? *(Pause.)* *(the smallest box, the first one)*

Put your finger on the number 9. Look at the picture of the shape. Which is the only other shape that will fit inside of it? *(Pause.)* *(the right-side-up cone)*

Put your finger on the number 10. Look at the picture of one shape inside another. What is the shape inside? Fill in the circle under your answer. *(Pause.)* *(the trapezoid)*

Put your finger on the number 11. Now you get to do some drawing. Listen carefully. On the blank line, draw a picture of a circle inside a triangle. *(Pause.)*

Put your finger on the number 12. Listen carefully. On the blank line, draw a picture of a square inside a circle. *(Pause.)*

Now stop.

ANSWER KEY

1. balloon **2.** zebra **3.** dress **4.** the fourth shape **5.** the fourth shape **6.** square
7. triangle **8.** the smallest box (the first shape) **9.** the right side up cone **10.** trapezoid
11. drawing of a circle inside a triangle **12.** drawing of square inside a circle

---

7.  | 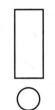 ○ 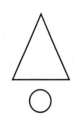 ○  ○  ○

8. | ○ ○ ○ ○

9.  | 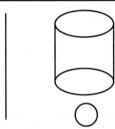 ○ 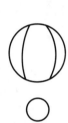 ○ 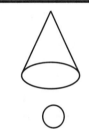 ○ ○

10. | ○  ○  ○

11.

_____

12.

_____

Science: Process

The important first grade science skills in this section include the following:

- making observations based on the five senses.
- classifying objects according to their properties.
- using amounts as a means of quantifying.
- estimating length, volume, mass, temperature.
- making inferences to form conclusions.
- making predictions.

Teacher Script

Look at the page. (*Check to make sure students are on the correct page.*) Things in the world are heavy, or soft, or hard. How do we learn about what is hard or soft or heavy? (*discussion*) This part of the test will ask what you know about the world by watching, listening, doing, and thinking. Here is a sample question at the top of your page.

See the pictures? Listen to my question. You can tell that something is hot or cold by using what part of your body? Fill in the circle under your answer. (*Pause.*) Which answer did you choose? (*hand*) Why? (*discussion*) This part of the book has questions like that.

Sample

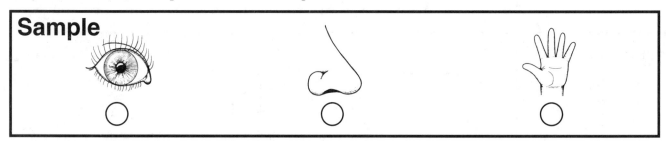

Now put your finger on the number 1. Here is the question. You can tell that a sound is loud or soft with what part of your body? (*Pause.*) (*ear*)

Put your finger on the number 2. You can tell that something is sweet or sour with what part of your body? Fill in the circle of your answer. (*Pause.*) (*mouth*)

Put your finger on the number 3. Here is a little story. You must listen carefully. Andrew came running down the street. "I could tell you were baking cookies," he told his mom. "How could you tell?" said his mother. "You were so far away." How could Andrew tell his mother was baking cookies? Fill in the circle of your answer. (*Pause.*) (*nose*)

Put your finger on the number 4. Here is another little story. Lauren said to Kristen, "Let's go! The parade is starting." Kristen said, "How do you know? I can't see it coming." How did Lauren know the parade was coming? (*Pause.*) (*ear*)

Put your finger on the number 5. Here is one more little story. Kyle and Luke were hiking. Kyle said, "I don't think I want to go to that hill over there. It's too far." Luke said, "How do you know it is far. You have never been there." How did Kyle know it was far to the hill? (*Pause.*) (*eye*)

Now stop.

ANSWER KEY

1. ear **2.** mouth **3.** nose **4.** ear **5.** eye

Sample

○   ○   ○

1.

   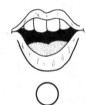

○   ○   ○

2.

○   ○   ○

3.

○   ○   ○

4.

○   ○   ○

5.

○   ○   ○

STOP

Teacher Script

Put your finger on the number 1. Here are three pictures. One of them doesn't belong because it is different. Which one doesn't belong? *(Pause.)* *(sun)*

Put your finger on the number 2. Here are three pictures again. One of them doesn't belong. Which one? *(Pause.)* *(car)*

Put your finger on the number 3. Here are three more pictures. One of these things doesn't belong. Which one? *(Pause.)* *(crayon)*

Put your finger on the number 4. Look at the three groups of birds. Which group has the most birds? Fill in the circle of your answer. *(Pause.)* *(third picture)*

Put your finger on the number 5. Look at the three bunches of balloons. Which bunch has the fewest balloons? *(Pause.)* *(second picture)*

Put your finger on the number 6. Here are pictures of three jars of buttons. Which jar is almost empty? *(Pause.)* *(second picture)*

Turn the page.

1.

○   ○   ○

2.

○   ○   ○

3.

○   ○   ○

4.

○   ○   ○

5.

   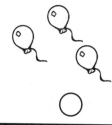

○   ○   ○

6.

○   ○   ○

Teacher Script *(cont.)*

Put your finger on the number 7. In this row, there are three pictures. Which one is the highest or tallest? *(Pause.)* *(door)*

Put your finger on the number 8. In this row there are also three pictures. Which one is the longest? *(Pause.)* *(snake)*

Put your finger on the number 9. Look at these pictures. Which one do you think is the hardest? *(Pause.)* *(rock)*

Put your finger on the number 10. Here are three pictures of rocks being weighed on a scale. Look carefully at the pictures. Which rock is the heaviest? Fill in the circle under your answer. *(Pause.)* *(third rock on the scale)*

Put your finger on the number 11. Now we are going to compare temperatures. Here are three thermometers. Which one shows the highest temperature? *(Pause.)* *(second thermometer)*

Put your finger on the number 12. Here is one more question about temperature. Here are pictures of ice, fire, and a glass of water. Which one would have the lowest temperature? *(Pause.)* *(ice)*

Now stop.

ANSWER KEY

1. sun **2.** car **3.** crayon **4.** the third group of birds **5.** the second bunch of balloons. **6.** the second jar of buttons **7.** door **8.** snake **9.** rock **10.** the third rock on scale **11.** the second thermometer **12.** ice

---

7.

◯　　　◯　　　◯

8.

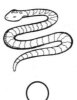

◯　　　◯　　　◯

9.

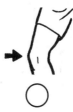  

◯　　　◯　　　◯

10.

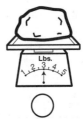 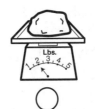 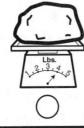

◯　　　◯　　　◯

11.

◯　　　◯　　　◯

12.

◯　　　◯　　　◯

STOP

Teacher Script

Put your finger on the number 1. Here are three boxes. Pretend that you want to save some crayons in one of these boxes. Which box would hold the most crayons? *(Pause.)* *(first one)*

Put your finger on the number 2. Each of these things has water in it. Which one would have the most water? *(Pause.)* *(fish tank)*

Put your finger on the number 3. Now I'm going to tell you a little story. You must guess what happened in the story. Here is the first one. I was having a cold drink with ice one hot summer day. I left my drink on the table outside. When I came back, the ice was gone. What happened to it? Choose the picture that shows what happened. *(Pause.)* *(the ice melting)*

Put your finger on the number 4. Here is another story. I bought a balloon. It floated and pulled a little on its string. Then, by accident, I let the string go. What happened to the balloon? Fill in the circle under your answer. *(Pause.)* *(balloon floating away)*

Put your finger on the number 5. Here is a picture of a fishbowl half filled with water. Then, for a joke, someone dropped a ball inside the fishbowl. Which picture shows what the fishbowl would look like after the ball has been dropped in it? *(Pause.)* *(water level is higher)*

Put your finger on the number 6. Here is the last story. Angela was making muffins. She poured them in a muffin tray and put the tray in the oven. But she did not turn the oven on. What will the muffins look like when she takes them out? *(Pause.)* *(second picture)*

Now stop.

ANSWER KEY

1. the biggest box (the first picture) **2.** fish tank **3.** ice cube melting **4.** balloon floating away **5.** water level is higher **6.** uncooked muffins (second picture)

1.

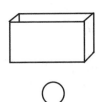

◯   ◯   ◯

2.

◯   ◯   ◯

3.

◯   ◯   ◯

4.

◯   ◯   ◯

5.

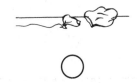 |       ◯

◯   ◯   ◯

6.

   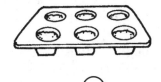   

◯   ◯   ◯

Social Studies: Individuals and Families

This section covers important first grade social studies skills including the following:

- identifying roles of individuals in the family.

- distinguishing similarities and differences among people.

- identifying social environments.

- comparing social environments.

- describing appropriate behaviors in various environments.

Teacher Script

This part of the book is about people. It is about families and how people live. There is a sample question at the top of your page. I am thinking of someone in a family. This person is very small. This person must be taken care of. This person is carried by other people in the family. Who is this person I'm thinking of? Fill in the circle of your answer. *(Pause.)* Which one did you choose? What were the clues? *(discussion)* Now you will listen while I give you other clues about families and people.

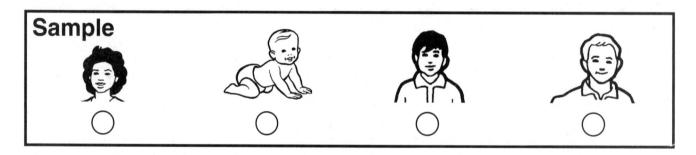

Sample

Put your finger on the number 1. Listen to my clues about people in a family. I have white hair. I babysit sometimes. The grownups in the family are my children. Which one is my picture? *(Pause.)* (*senior citizen*)

Put your finger on the number 2. Here are the clues. I take care of my brother who is a little baby. I am older than he is. I am in elementary school. Which one is my picture? *(Pause.)* (*girl*)

Put your finger on the number 3. I use a special way to go from place to place because I cannot walk. Which is my picture? *(Pause.)* (*person in wheelchair*)

Put your finger on the number 4. Now I am going to ask you about people you see. Look at the pictures. Which picture shows people sharing? *(Pause.)* (*third picture*)

Put your finger on the number 5. Look at the pictures. Who is dressed in a sari? *(Pause.)* (*first picture*)

Turn the page.

Sample.

○   ○   ○   ○

1.

○   ○   ○   ○

2.

○   ○   ○

3.

○   ○   ○

4.

○   ○   ○

5.

○   ○   ○   ○

Teacher Script *(cont.)*

Now here are some questions about how to act or behave in different places.

Put your finger on the number 6. Look at the pictures. Where is a place where you can cheer and shout? *(Pause.)* *(soccer game)*

Put your finger on the number 7. Look at the pictures. Which is a picture of behavior in school? *(Pause.)* *(child raising hand)*

Put your finger on the number 8. Look at the pictures. Which is a picture of a place where you must be quiet and respectful. *(Pause.)* *(church)*

Put your finger on the number 9. Look at the pictures. Which is a picture of a place where you must thank people and share? *(Pause.)* *(birthday party)*

Put your finger on the number 10. Where is a place where you must cooperate and take your turn? *(Pause.)* *(participating in a game)*

Now stop.

ANSWER KEY

1. senior citizen **2.** girl **3.** person in the wheelchair **4.** children sharing ball **5.** first picture
6. soccer game **7.** child raising hand **8.** church **9.** birthday party **10.** participating in a game

---

6.

    ◯   ◯   ◯

7.

    ◯   ◯   ◯

8.

    ◯   ◯   ◯

9.

  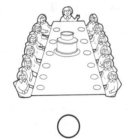

    ◯   ◯   ◯

10.

    ◯   ◯   ◯

STOP

Social Studies: Authority and Responsibility

This section reviews important first grade social studies skills including the following:

- identifying individuals who have authority.

- recognizing the consequences of responsible and irresponsible actions.

Teacher Script

Now we will answer some questions about people we must obey. And we will answer questions about safe and unsafe behavior.

Put your finger on the number 1. Look at the pictures of the three adults. Which one is a referee who makes sure a game is fair? *(Pause.)* *(second one)*

Put your finger on the number 2. Look at the pictures. Which one is a police car? *(Pause.)* *(the first one)*

Put your finger on the number 3. Listen to my question. Which picture shows a man who is a leader of a church? *(Pause.)* *(third one)*

Put your finger on the number 4. Here are three pictures of children doing things. Which picture shows children being safe? *(Pause.)* *(second one)*

Put your finger on the number 5. Here are three more pictures of children doing things. Which picture shows a child being unsafe? *(Pause.)* *(third one)*

Put your finger on the 6. Look at these pictures of children. Which one shows a child disobeying? *(Pause.)* *(the first one)*

Now stop.

ANSWER KEY

1. referee (the second picture) 2. police car (the first picture) 3. the minister (the third picture) 4. adult supervising children wearing life vests in the water 5. child swimming away from the shore 6. child running around pool

---

Social Studies: Authority and Responsibility (cont.)

1.

   ◯   ◯   ◯

2.

   ◯   ◯   ◯

3.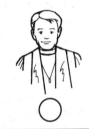

   ◯   ◯   ◯

4.

   ◯   ◯   ◯

5.

   ◯   ◯   ◯

6.

   ◯   ◯   ◯

Social Studies: Religious and Cultural Traditions

This first grade social studies skills section includes the following:

- identifying religious and secular symbols.

- identifying symbols associated with holidays.

Teacher Script

Now we need to think about our country and how we live in the United States.

Put your finger on the number 1. In this row are pictures of flags. Which flag stands for the United States of America? *(Pause.)* *(second flag)*

Put your finger on the number 2. Here are some pictures of things. One of these you will most likely see by a church. Which one? Fill in the circle of your answer. *(Pause.)* *(cross)*

Put your finger on the number 3. Listen carefully. St. Patrick's Day is a celebration in March. Many people wear green. Which picture will you see on St. Patrick's Day? *(Pause.)* *(shamrock)*

Put your finger on the number 4. Look at the words in this row. There is another holiday when the United States celebrates its birthday with fireworks. What is the date of this celebration? *(Pause.)* *(July 4)*

Put your finger on the number 5. Every year for Halloween children dress up to go trick or treating. Which one of the pictures in this row might you see on Halloween? *(Pause.)* *(jack-o'-lantern)*

Put your finger on the number 6. Here are pictures of three popular games in the United States. Which one is played in the summertime? *(Pause.)* *(baseball)*

Turn the page.

Social Studies: Religious and Cultural Traditions *(cont.)*

1.

2.

3.

4.

December 25   **January 1**   **July 4**

5.

6.

Teacher Script *(cont.)*

Put your finger on the number 7. There is a sign that means "no." Which one of these signs means "no"? *(Pause.)* *(circle with a slash)*

Put your finger on the number 8. Here are some things used for celebrations. One of them is used by people who are Jewish to celebrate Hanukkah. Which one? *(Pause.)* *(the menorah)*

Put your finger on the number 9. Which pictures shows what people do with their hands when they pray? *(Pause.)* *(second picture)*

Put your finger on the number 10. Here are more pictures of hands. Which one shows people shaking hands? *(Pause.)* *(first picture)*

Put your finger on the number 11. There is a famous statue in the United States. It is the Statue of Liberty. Which picture shows the Statue of Liberty? *(Pause.)* *(third one)*

Put your finger on the number 12. Our country has a national bird. This bird symbolizes courage and freedom. Which picture shows this bird? *(Pause.)* *(third one)*

Now we stop.

ANSWER KEY

1. second flag **2.** cross **3.** shamrock **4.** July 4 **5.** jack-o'-lantern **6.** baseball **7.** circle with a slash **8.** menorah **9.** hands together (second picture) **10.** hands shaking (first picture) **11.** Statue of Liberty (third picture) **12.** bald eagle (third picture)

7.

STOP ○   ○   ○

8.

○   ○   ○

9.

○   ○   ○

10.

○   ○   ○

11.

○   ○   ○

12.

○   ○   ○

First grade social studies skills in this section include the following:

- locating familiar places in the home, classroom, and school.

- identifying functions of places in homes and schools.

- analyzing patterns of movement between homes and schools.

Teacher Script

We all live places, and we all come to school. The questions in this last part of the test are about where we live and go to school.

Put your finger on the number 1. Look at the pictures. Which picture shows what you would do in the kitchen or dining room of a house? Fill in the circle of your answer. *(Pause.)* *(have a meal)*

Put your finger on the number 2. Look at the pictures. Which is something you will find in a kitchen? *(Pause.)* *(a stove)*

Put your finger on the number 3. Look at the pictures. Which picture shows what you would do in the bedroom of a house? *(Pause.)* *(sleep)*

Put your finger on the number 4. Which picture shows what you would do outside a house? *(Pause.)* *(play an outdoor game)*

Put your finger on the number 5. Which picture shows children on their way to school? Fill in the circle of your answer. *(Pause.)* *(children walking with books)*

Put your finger on the number 6. Which picture shows how you might get to school if you had far to go? Fill in the circle of your answer. *(Pause.)* *(bus)*

Turn the page.

1.       

◯   ◯   ◯

2.    

◯   ◯   ◯

3.       

◯   ◯   ◯

4.       

◯   ◯   ◯

5.       

◯   ◯   ◯

6.    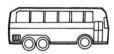   

◯   ◯   ◯

Teacher Script *(cont.)*

Put your finger on the number 7. Look at the pictures. Which is something you might see in a school? *(Pause.)* *(a globe)*

Put your finger on the number 8. Which picture shows something I, the teacher, might do at school? *(Pause.)* *(read a story)*

Put your finger on the number 9. Which picture shows a child in a library at school? *(Pause.)* *(the first one)*

Put your finger on the number 10. Now I want you to draw a picture. Use the rest of the page to draw your picture. *(You can distribute crayons if that is how the students usually draw.)* Draw a picture of you sitting in our class. You can show other things to give an idea of where you sit, like where the door is or where the windows are. *(Allow students about 15 minutes for the activity. In the finished picture, there should be signs—"landmarks"—that indicate the child has a sense of direction and his or her relative location.)*

Stop after you finish your drawing.

ANSWER KEY

1. have a meal **2.** stove **3.** sleep **4.** play an outdoor game **5.** children walking with books **6.** bus **7.** globe **8.** read a story **9.** first picture **10.** Drawings will vary.

7.

○   ○   ○

8.

○   ○   ○

9.

○   ○   ○

10.

Tips for Parents: Help Your Child to Write Well

Children must be ready to learn from the first day of school. And of course, preparing children for school is a historic responsibility of parents.

Should you help your child with writing? Yes, if you want your child to do well in school, enjoy self-expression, and become more self-reliant. You know how important writing will be to your child's life. It will be important from first grade through college and throughout adulthood. After all, writing is . . .

Practical

Most of us make lists, jot down reminders, and write notes and instructions at least occasionally.

Job-Related

Professional and white-collar workers write frequently—preparing memos, letters, briefing papers, sales reports, articles, research reports, or proposals. Most workers do some kind of writing on the job.

Stimulating

Writing helps to provoke thoughts and to organize them logically and concisely.

Social

Most of us—at least occasionally—write thank-you notes and letters to friends.

Therapeutic

It can be helpful to express feelings in writing that cannot be expressed so easily by speaking.

How You Can Help

1. **Encourage your child to draw and to discuss his or her drawings.** One of the first means of communication for your child is through drawing. Ask questions such as the following: *What is the boy doing? Does the house look like ours? Can you tell a story about this picture?*

2. **Show an interest in and ask questions about the things your child says, draws, and may try to write.** Most children's basic speech patterns are formed by the time they enter school. By that time, children speak clearly, recognize most letters of the alphabet, and may try to write.

3. **Make it real.** Your child also needs to do real writing. It is more important for the child to write a letter to a relative than it is to write a one-line note on a greeting card. Encourage your child to write to relatives and friends. Perhaps your child would enjoy corresponding with a pen pal.

Tips for Parents: Help Your Child to Write Well *(cont.)*

How You Can Help *(cont.)*

4. **Suggest note-taking.** Encourage your child to take notes on trips or outings and to describe what he or she saw. This could include a description of nature walks, a boat ride, a car trip, or other events that lend themselves to note-taking.

5. **Brainstorm.** Talk with your child as much as possible about his/her impressions and encourage the child to describe people and events to you. If the child's description is especially accurate and colorful, say so.

6. **Write together.** Have your child help you with letters, even such routine ones as ordering items from an advertisement or writing to a business firm. This helps the child to see firsthand that writing is important to adults and truly useful.

7. **Use games.** There are numerous games and puzzles that help a child to increase vocabulary and make a child more fluent in speaking and writing. Remember that building a vocabulary builds confidence. Try crossword puzzles, word games, anagrams, and cryptograms designed especially for children. Flash cards are good, too, and they are easy to make at home.

8. **Suggest making lists.** Most children like to make lists just as they like to count. Making lists is good practice and helps a child to become more organized. Boys and girls might make lists of their records, tapes, baseball cards, dolls, furniture in a room, etc. They could include items they want. It is also good practice to make lists of things to do, schoolwork, dates for tests, social events, and other reminders.

9. **Encourage copying.** If a child likes a particular song, suggest learning the words by writing them down—replaying the song on your CD player or jotting down the words whenever the song is played on a radio program. Also encourage copying favorite poems or quotations from books and plays. Overall, if you show a positive and interested attitude toward writing, your child will, too.

I liked the beach.

The sand was hot.

Tips for Parents: Help Your Child with Math

It is highly likely that when you studied math, you were expected to complete lots of problems accurately and quickly. There was only one way to arrive at your answers, and it was believed that the best way to improve math ability was to do more problems and to do them fast. Today, the focus is less on the quantity of memorized problems and more on understanding the concepts and applying thinking skills to arrive at an answer. While accuracy is always important, a wrong answer may help you and your child discover what your child may not understand. You might find some of the following thoughts helpful when thinking about wrong answers.

- **Realize problems can be solved in different ways.** While problems in math may have only one solution, there may be many ways to get the right answer. When working on math problems with your child, ask, "Could you tell me how you got that answer?" Your child's way might be different from yours. If the answer is correct and the strategy or way of solving it has worked, it is a great alternative. By encouraging children to talk about what they are thinking, we help them to become stronger mathematicians and independent thinkers.

- **Realize doing math in your head is important.** Have you ever noticed that today very few people take their pencil and paper out to solve problems in the grocery, fast food, or department store or in the office? Instead, most people estimate in their heads. Calculators and computers demand that people put in the correct information and that they know if the answers are reasonable. Usually, people look at the answer to determine if it makes sense, applying the math in their heads to the problem. This is the reason why doing math in their heads is so important to our children as they enter the 21st century.

How You Can Help

1. **Help your child do mental math with lots of small numbers in their heads until they develop quick and accurate responses.** Questions such as, "If I have 4 cups, and I need 7 cups, how many more do I need?" or "If I need 12 drinks for the class, how many packages of 3 drinks will I need to buy?"

2. **Encourage your child to estimate the answer.** When estimating, try to use numbers to make it easy to solve problems quickly in your head to determine a reasonable answer. For example, when figuring 18 plus 29, an easy way to get a "close" answer is to think about 20 + 30 = [?].

Tips for Parents: Help Your Child with Math *(cont.)*

How You Can Help *(cont.)*

3. **Allow your child to use strategies that make sense to him or her.** Ask often, "Is your answer reasonable? Is it reasonable that you added 17 and 35 and got 367? Why? Why not?"

4. **Ask your child to explain how the problem was solved.** The response might help you discover if your child needs help with the procedures, the number facts, or the concepts involved. Sometimes the wrong answer to a problem might be because the child thinks the problem is asking another question. For example, when children see the problem 4 + __ = 9, they often respond with an answer of 13. They think the problem is asking "What is 4 + 9?" instead of "4 plus what missing number amount equals 9?"

   You may have learned something the teacher might find helpful. A short note or call will alert the teacher to possible ways of helping your child.

5. **Help your child be a risk taker.** Help him or her see the value of examining a wrong answer, and assure him or her that the right answers will come with proper understanding.

6. **Emphasize that math is enjoyable and practical.** Math is part of the everyday world. Even when you are at a fast-food restaurant, point to the prices on the menu and say, "Look! More numbers—they are everywhere!"

Above all, be patient. All children want to succeed. They do not want red marks or incorrect answers. They want to be proud and to make you and the teacher proud. So, the wrong answer tells you to look further, to ask questions, and to see what the wrong answer is saying about the child's understanding.

$$4 + 3 = 7$$

$$\begin{array}{r} 9 \\ + 1 \\ \hline 10 \end{array}$$

$$2 + 3 = 5$$

$$\begin{array}{r} 8 \\ + 0 \\ \hline 8 \end{array}$$

$$\begin{array}{r} 7 \\ + 5 \\ \hline 12 \end{array}$$

$$6 + 3 = 9$$

Tips for Parents: Help Your Child with Reading

You are your child's first teacher. According to the National Institute of Education, the most important thing you can do to help your child succeed in school is to read aloud to him or her. Reading to your child makes them feel respected and part of your world. It builds self-esteem.

Reading aloud to your child stimulates the mind, strengthens the imagination, and makes your child curious about the world. Reading aloud will help him or her to understand words, master language, and enable him or her to arrive at school feeling confident.

How You Can Help

1. **Make the reading time special.** Turn off the TV, radio, or anything that will distract from your time together. Story time can be a special part of every day—before bedtime or after a nap. Be responsive at other times, too, if your child brings a book and needs quiet time with you.

2. **Patience!** Reading to children takes time, but you will be letting them know how important they are to you. Children also love to read favorite books over and over again. Being comfortable with a book gives them confidence.

3. **Have your child choose the book you will be reading together.** Sit close together. Hold the book so your child can see it, and let him or her turn the pages.

4. **Take time to look at the pictures and talk about them.** Ask your child what he or she thinks is happening or what the characters are feeling.

5. **Make the story come to life by reading with expression.** Change your voice to become different characters or to fit different situations (deep/low, quiet/soft). Ask your child to make special sounds with you—a growling animal or a howling wind.

6. **Stop at interesting points in the story and ask questions** such as "What do you think will happen next?" or "What would you do if you were there?" Help your child relate the story to his or her own experiences by asking questions like "Have you ever felt that way?" Listening to what your child has to say lets him or her know that his or her thoughts are important to you.

7. **Have fun with books and language.** Play games, sing songs, and create rhymes with your children. Read books that offer funny situations and characters so you can enjoy them and laugh together.

8. **Finally, the library can be a familiar and special place for you and your child.** Obtain a library card in your child's name. This will build self-esteem and give him or her a sense of involvement.